MACHINE QUILTING
WITH STYLE

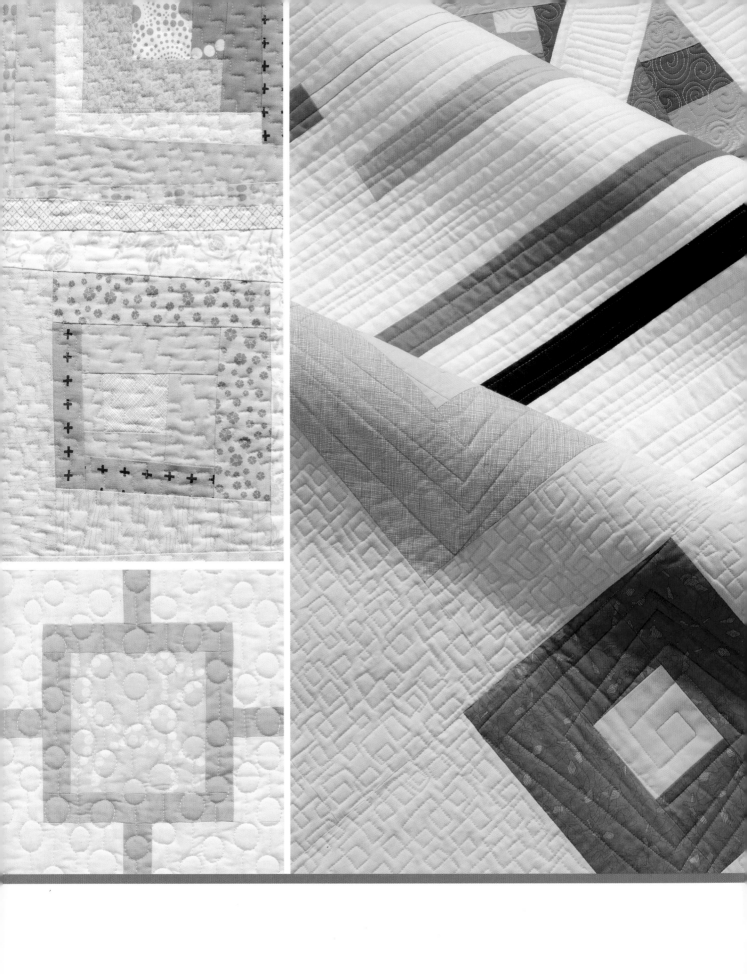

MACHINE QUILTING
WITH STYLE
From Walking-Foot Wonders to Free-Motion Favorites

Christa Watson

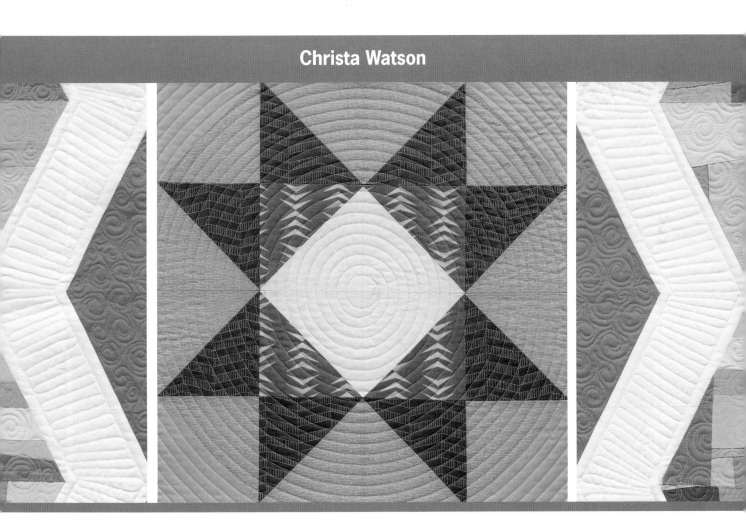

Martingale®
Create with Confidence

Dedication

To the love of my life—my husband, Jason. He has always been my greatest fan and supporter. Even when we went through a period of time when "Christa didn't quilt," he was always there, cheering me on. My very first quilt was made for him many years ago, and he's been encouraging me in my quilting efforts ever since.

And to my three wonderful children: Jason Jr., Ryan, and Jenna. They put up with the craziness that a quilter's life brings. I'm so glad I've been able to make quilts for them throughout the years.

Machine Quilting with Style: From Walking-Foot Wonders to Free-Motion Favorites
© 2015 by Christa Watson

Martingale®
19021 120th Ave. NE, Ste. 102
Bothell, WA 98011-9511 USA
ShopMartingale.com

Printed in China
20 19 18 17 16 15   8 7 6 5 4 3 2 1

**Library of Congress Cataloging-in-Publication Data
is available upon request.**

ISBN: 978-1-60468-625-8

MISSION STATEMENT

Dedicated to providing quality products and service to inspire creativity.

CREDITS

PUBLISHER AND CHIEF VISIONARY OFFICER
Jennifer Erbe Keltner

EDITORIAL DIRECTOR
Karen Costello Soltys

ACQUISITIONS EDITOR
Karen M. Burns

TECHNICAL EDITOR
Laurie Baker

COPY EDITOR
Sheila Chapman Ryan

DESIGN DIRECTOR
Paula Schlosser

PHOTOGRAPHER
Brent Kane

PRODUCTION MANAGER
Regina Girard

COVER AND
INTERIOR DESIGNER
Adrienne Smitke

ILLUSTRATOR
Lisa Lauch

Thanks to Quiltworks Northwest in Bellevue, Washington, for allowing us to take machine-quilting photos (pages 12 and 13) in their shop.

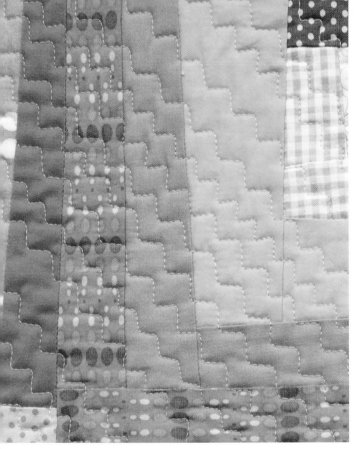

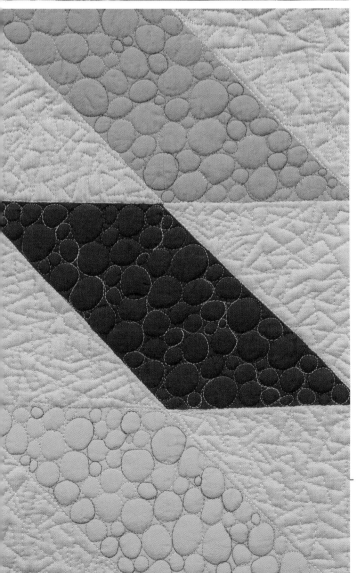

Contents

Introduction

I love quilting my own quilts! In fact, I enjoy every step of the quiltmaking process and I love it when quilts are used. I also firmly believe that quilts don't have to be perfect to be both functional and beautiful. Where there's a will to quilt, there's definitely a way.

In this book, I'm excited to share with you 12 original patterns with step-by-step instructions on how to quilt them on your home sewing machine. The projects have been organized into two categories: "Walking-Foot Wonders" and "Free-Motion Favorites." First, I'll show you the mechanics of how to quilt each design on a practice sample, and then I'll encourage you to try out the motifs on an actual quilt. And just for fun, I pieced a couple of the quilt backs and included those instructions too! I also share my favorite methods of basting (it's not as bad as you think) and how to finish your quilts with style.

I encourage you to learn and practice at your own pace and enjoy the tremendous journey you're on. Have fun with both the piecing *and* the quilting, and please feel free to mix up the ideas presented for your own unique take on a quilt design. Above all, please don't get hung up on perfection. After completing any of the quilts in this book, I hope that you'll feel immense satisfaction in proclaiming, "I made it myself!"

~ *Christa*

YOU Can Be the Quilter

The concern I hear most often in my quilting classes is, "I don't have a fancy machine. How can I quilt my own quilt?" My answer is that the most important tool you need for successful machine quilting is a can-do attitude. Often it's my students with the least expensive machines that have the most success. What these students lacked in bells-and-whistles features they made up for in determination and creativity. My first machine was pretty bare-bones, yet I still quilted successfully with it using many of the techniques I'll show you. It's taken me nearly 20 years to afford the machine of my dreams (a Bernina 710), yet if I'd waited until I had the perfect machine, I would never have gained the experience I needed to write this book.

Along with confidence and a positive attitude, you'll benefit from reading through the following information about batting and threads, how to press seam allowances to make quilting easier, and how to set up your machine and work area for the quilting process. This basic knowledge will prepare you to dive into the techniques that follow and ensure you're on your way to successfully quilting your quilts on your home sewing machine.

BATTING CHOICES

The batting you use has a huge effect on the look and feel of your quilt, and it plays a role in how easy or difficult quilting will be. Some factors to consider are fiber content, loft, thickness, color, and how to launder the finished quilt to maintain the integrity of the batting.

Quilt batting is available in many different fibers and blends. After much trial and error, I've found that I have the best success machine quilting when using batting made from natural fibers like cotton, silk, or bamboo. Synthetic batting made from polyester or recycled plastic bottles, is very slippery and seems to cause more bunching and puckering. Of course, your results may vary, but this is what works for me. Ultimately, the best way to see how battings perform is to try them and see what works for you.

I used different battings for each of the 12 quilts in this book, including cotton, wool, soy, bamboo, silk, and a combination of blends. I've listed the batting used in the "Quilt Details" box included with each project. Here are a few of my favorites:

Cotton. A high-quality, thin (or low-loft) cotton batting is by far the easiest batting to work with for quilting on a home sewing machine. Cotton fabrics naturally cling to cotton batting and there's very little

■ Battings come in a range of colors, including white, natural, or black (not pictured).

shifting, which means few (if any) puckers and tucks. Cotton battings soften up wash after wash, but they do tend to shrink quite a bit initially. Fortunately, the shrinkage gives your quilt a nice antique, crinkled look. This is an added benefit when you're just starting your machine-quilting adventures because the texture created from the shrinkage can hide a multitude of mistakes! Cotton batting is available in different lofts. Basting spray (see page 106) clings well to cotton batting when basting the quilt layers together.

Wool. Next to cotton, this is my second favorite batting fiber. It's very lightweight and warm in the winter yet cool in the summer. Wool has memory, which means it springs back into shape after folding, making it an ideal choice for show quilts or those that will be folded often. It has a higher loft than cotton so it can really highlight your quilting. The downside is that it's more costly than cotton and it can give off an odor when wet. Some people may also be allergic to wool.

Blends. Most of the other battings I used in this book are blends of fibers, such as soy, silk, or bamboo mixed with cotton or another primary fiber. The blends are nice because they give the best properties of each material. One of my favorite blends is cotton and wool; it provides the drape and economy of cotton with the memory and loft of wool. Make your own by layering a cotton and wool batting together, placing the wool on the top and the cotton on the bottom.

When considering the loft, or thickness, of your quilt, remember that fiber content will affect loft and each will perform differently. Low-loft battings appear flatter than high-loft battings, so if you're looking for "poof," choose a thicker loft or combine layers of thin battings to create the desired look. Low-loft cotton batting will drape differently than low-loft polyester batting. Also keep in mind the end use; for a wall hanging, you'll want more structure and less drape, so consider a firmer batting. A baby quilt that will require frequent washings is a good candidate for a lightweight batting (preferably flame retardant). Large bed-size quilts are easier to manipulate under your machine when you use a low-loft batting.

Batting also comes in different colors, but not all batting types come in all colors. The three most common colors are natural, white, or black, but black is available in fewer options. Select a color that won't change the color of the fabrics on the quilt top or back when they're layered together.

Before you purchase any batting, read the manufacturer's information for prewashing and for the maximum distance you can leave between quilting stitches and still maintain the structural integrity of the batting.

Try These Tips for Wrinkle Removal

- Spread out your batting a day or two before use to let it relax.
- Toss your batting in the dryer with a damp towel.
- You can iron most cotton battings; be sure to test them first!

THOUGHTS ON THREAD

The threads you use will affect the finished look of your quilt. Like batting, thread comes in different fibers and weights, and each combination can produce a different result. Some threads sink into the quilt and blend in with the fabrics, while others lie on top and steal the show. Stitch a sample to help you determine which thread will give you the desired result. Use the same fabrics and batting for your sample that you'll use in your quilt top to get a true idea of the finished look.

Always buy the best thread you can afford. Using high-quality, low-lint thread for quilting is just as important as it is for piecing. My favorite thread for both piecing and quilting is Aurifil 100% cotton in 50 weight. It remains soft to the touch, even when used for densely quilted areas. Cotton thread blends well, and leftovers can be used for piecing scrappy quilts. Fine silk threads will also blend into the quilt and are especially nice for doing micro-stippling. However, silk thread is pricey, so you may want to save it for quilting small projects or heirloom pieces. I've also had success using a variety of polyester threads for decorative machine quilting. Clear monofilament and metallic threads provide interesting results, but they are harder to work with. Try a variety of threads from different manufacturers to see which threads you (and your machine) prefer.

When you want the quilting to be the star, choose a thicker thread for the top. The lower the thread-weight number, the thicker it is. So, 40 weight is thicker than 50 weight and will stand out more. If you want the thread to take even more of the spotlight, try a 28 weight.

Thread color is also important. A color that blends with the colors in the quilt will allow the fabrics and quilt pattern to shine, whereas a thread that contrasts with the fabrics will emphasize the quilting.

Match the bobbin thread color to the needle thread color whenever possible. However, the thread weights do not have to match. A 50-weight thread in the bobbin generally produces good results, and you can fit more thread onto the bobbin than with a heavier thread, which means fewer bobbin changes.

Use a machine needle to match the weight of the top thread: use an 80/12 needle with a 50-weight thread, a 90/14 needle with a 40-weight thread, and a 100/16 needle with a 28-weight thread. For machine quilting, I use topstitch needles, Sharps, or needles specifically labeled for machine quilting.

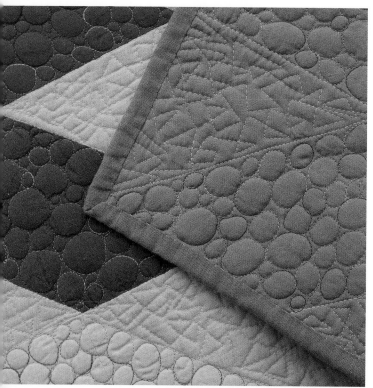

■ "Broken V" (page 85) uses matching and contrasting threads effectively in the same quilt.

PRESSING

While pressing generally goes hand in hand with piecing a quilt top, the direction the seam allowances are pressed can affect how your quilt looks when it's finished. And it can impact how easy or difficult it is to quilt your project. So, take pressing seriously!

I prefer to press my seam allowances open using a dry iron so as not to distort the seam. Pressing the seam allowances open is more time-consuming than pressing them to one side, however, it does two things for me that more than make up for the effort: First, I don't have to constantly worry which way to press the seam allowances to make sure they abut. This saves me a lot of thinking time and aggravation. The second (and hugely important) reason is that open seam allowances create flatter blocks, which really aids in machine quilting. The quickest way to break a needle while quilting is to repeatedly stitch over lumps and bumps in your quilt. If you're concerned about your seams splitting when you press them open, use a smaller stitch length when piecing.

When pressing short seam allowances, nudge them open with the tip of your iron. When pressing longer seam allowances, open them with your fingertips and then gently press with your fingers or a wooden seam-roller tool. Follow up by pressing the open seam allowances with an iron.

■ Finger-press seams open, and then press with a dry iron.

MACHINE-QUILTING SETUP

Work surface, ergonomics, and hand position all play a part in making the quilting process smooth and enjoyable. When quilting on a home machine, the surface you work on should be even with the bed of your machine, and you should have as much work surface behind and to the left of your machine as possible. This will help hold the weight of the quilt, give your arms a surface to rest on, and eliminate drag, which can cause uneven stitching. A drop-in sewing table is an excellent investment if you'll be quilting a lot of quilts. I'd venture to say that the table is even more important than the machine! Drop-in sewing tables feature an opening the machine sits into so the machine bed is flush with the table surface. Custom-made inserts are available to fit around the machine to cover the opening. If you don't want to purchase a table, consider cutting an opening large enough for your machine from a sturdy

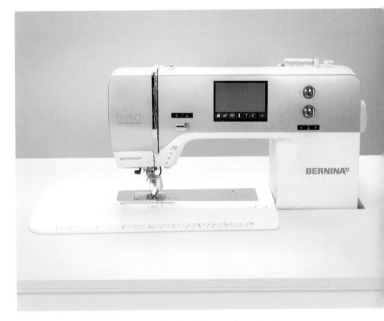

■ Most drop-in tables can be fitted with a custom insert made specifically for your machine.

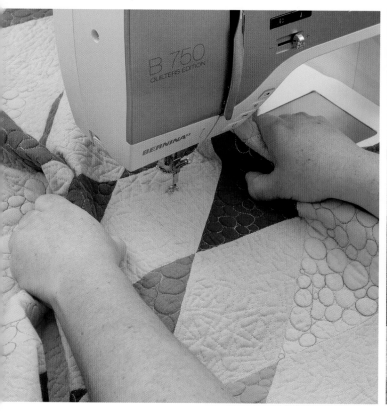

■ Some people like to "drive" their quilt by grasping the edges of the quilt with their hands while they stitch.

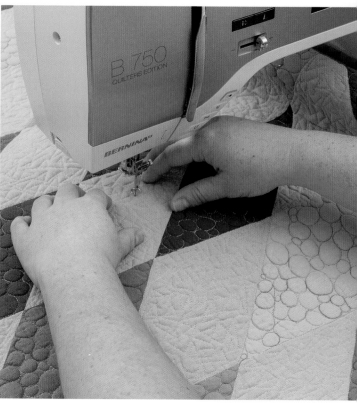

■ Others like to tiptoe over the top by using their fingertips to gently guide their quilt under the needle.

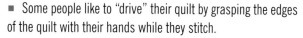

table. Position a tray to hold the machine inside the opening at a level that places the bed flush with the machine in the same manner that a drop-in table does. Fit the opening with a custom-made insert so you have a completely flat surface area on which to work.

If you work on a surface where the level of the machine can't be adjusted, such as your dining room table, you have other options. You can build up the area around the base of the machine instead. Many companies make acrylic extension tables that slide into position around the machine to create the same effect as having a drop-in table *and* give you more work surface. Or get creative and use Styrofoam or books to add additional height behind and to the left of the machine. It's also helpful if you can position another table to your left, creating an L shape.

An adjustable-height ironing board works in a pinch, as does a portable tray table.

Once your work surface is set up, make sure your body and hands are positioned correctly. Quilting ergonomics are very important: your feet should rest comfortably on the floor with your arms resting comfortably on the bed of your machine. If you have to quilt in less-than-ideal circumstances, be sure to take breaks often and stretch. I find that if I quilt for more than two hours at a time, my neck and arms can become stiff and sore, which means it's time to move on to something else.

When quilting, try to "puddle" the quilt by scrunching up the area around where you're quilting so that your immediate work space is flat and moves freely. Stop often and reposition both your hands and the quilt to keep it feeding smoothly under the

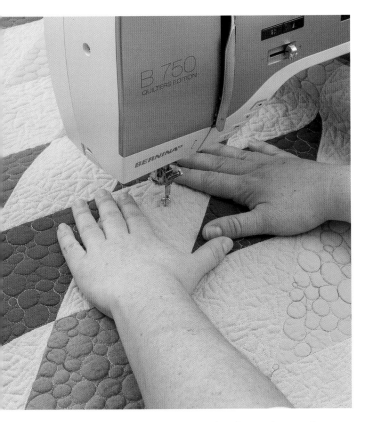

Where to Start Quilting

Each project in this book includes quilting suggestions. If your quilt is well basted (page 106), you can begin quilting in the middle or from the side, depending on the quilt design.

Find Your Hand Position

Each of the hand positions shown at left yields good results. Try each to see which feels more comfortable and natural to you. I don't use a hoop for quilting; it just gets in my way.

■ I'm most comfortable using my hands as a hoop, palms flat on the quilt, using the weight of my hands to move the quilt around.

quilting foot at all times. Position the quilt so that the least amount of bulk is under the arm of the quilt at one time. Don't be afraid to rotate or squish your quilt as needed to get the bulk out of the way as much as possible. I call this the "scrunch and smoosh" method of dealing with the bulk.

There are products available that will aid you in the machine-quilting process. I like to use quilting gloves that give me an extra bit of grip on the quilt, allowing me to control the movement. When free-motion quilting, I also use a slick silicon mat that temporarily sticks to the bed of my machine, making for a more slippery work surface and easier movement. If you can't drop your feed dogs for free-motion quilting (or if you get better tension when they're up), the mat also serves to cover up the feed dogs so you can freely move the quilt in all directions.

■ Rather than rolling or folding the quilt neatly, I "scrunch and smoosh" it out of the way as needed.

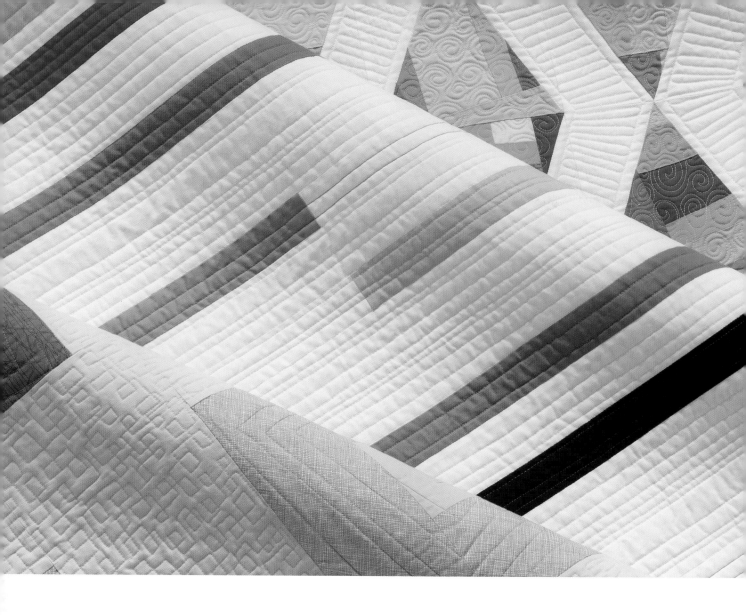

Walking-Foot Wonders

Quilting with a walking foot or built-in even-feed foot (also called a dual-feed foot) is usually the first technique brand-new quilters try. It's a great way to get your feet wet with quilting (pun intended)! Stitching in the ditch may be the first thing you think of when using a walking foot, but don't think you're limited to that technique. Here you'll find eight designs that you can use to quilt your projects with a walking foot—and not all of them are straight lines!

For each design, create a practice quilt sandwich made from two 10" squares of fabric with a layer of batting between them. Quilt each design separately, taking note of tension settings and stitch lengths. This is a great time to try out different battings, threads, and marking techniques.

■ A walking foot with an open toe gives great visibility.

DECORATIVE STITCHES

Use a serpentine stitch, also known as an altered running stitch, or other decorative stitch on your machine to create an interesting design. It's a great way to add texture to the surface of an entire quilt without having to match your quilting thread exactly to your fabric. Experiment with both length and width settings to find a design that you like. Try stitching in multiple directions, adding more or fewer lines of quilting for different effects.

When quilting with a decorative stitch, be sure you understand how the stitch is formed in case you need to rotate the quilt to continue the stitch pattern. Stitch slowly and allow the machine to do the work. If the design starts to skew or bunch up, that means you have too much drag or friction on the quilt.

Once you find a stitch you like, try to find two or three more for variety. Or try combining multiple stitches for added interest.

PARALLEL LINES

Long lines of quilting are actually harder to keep perfectly straight than you might think, so I prefer to call them "not-so-straight" lines. Whatever you call them, they're fun and quick to stitch! Perfect symmetry isn't necessary when quilting parallel lines; try varying the amount of space between lines for an industrial look. Parallel lines look great as an allover quilting design, or use them as a background filler in the negative space of your quilts. When parallel lines are spaced ⅛" apart or closer, it's also known as matchstick quilting.

A ruler and removable pencil or marker can be used for marking lines to follow on your quilt top, but there are other options available.

- A *hera* is a Japanese tool that marks by making an indentation as it's pulled across the fabric. Marks are easier to see if they're made after the quilt has been layered, and they're easily removed by misting with water.

- Painter's tape is low tack and comes in many different widths. It can be used on the fabric without harming it, although you shouldn't leave it on your quilt for long periods of time. Place the tape on the quilt top and stitch right along the straight edge, and then remove the tape when your line is stitched.

- The edge of your quilting foot can be used to follow a previously stitched line. Establish the first line of quilting using one of the methods above, and then follow it with the edge of the walking foot for the next line. This is an easy way to stitch rows of consistently spaced lines, although some machines will allow you to adjust the needle position to stitch lines of various width spacing as well.

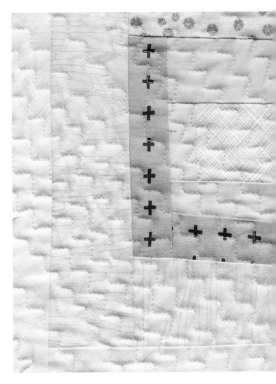

■ Detail of a decorative stitch on "Ripples" (page 22)

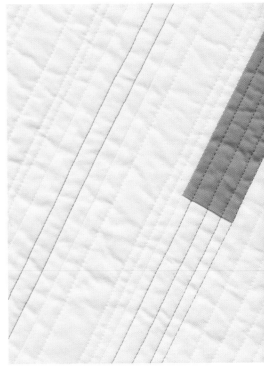

■ Detail of parallel lines on "Rain" (page 28)

Try quilting several straight or not-so-straight parallel lines on your practice quilting sandwich. Start with a thread color to match your fabric and begin stitching on one side of the sandwich, quilting each line from top to bottom. Vary the width of your spacing using your walking foot as a guide if you can, or mark lines with tape and quilt along the edges. After you've quilted a few lines with matching thread, switch to a contrasting thread and quilt a few more lines for a different effect. Add horizontal and diagonal lines to your practice piece, keeping them roughly parallel. Rotate the quilt as needed so you're always stitching from top to bottom.

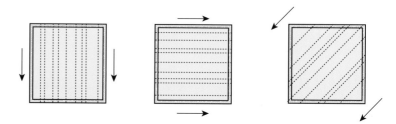

LINEAR ECHOES

Make your free-motion quilting pop by echoing the major seam lines ¼" to ½" away from the seam using a walking foot to outline your work. First, stitch in the ditch to secure your shape. To quilt the echo line, keep the edge of your presser foot next to the seamline at all times, stopping to pivot and turn the quilt if needed.

For this practice piece, use a leftover block that has several seams for the top layer of your sandwich and quilt linear echoes next to the seams in matching thread. Or, draw a geometric shape representing your block on a piece of plain fabric and echo quilt one or more lines around it.

When quilting linear echoes, try to quilt the longest continuous line that you can. If your line stops at a border or sashing, consider continuing the quilting through the border or sashing in the same pattern for an interesting, decorative effect.

■ Detail of linear echoes combined with free-motion quilting on "Facets" (page 90)

RADIATING LINES

Straight lines radiating from a single point or a variety of points can create incredible movement in your quilt. Mark and quilt a series of straight lines, starting at or near one corner of your practice piece. Don't worry about keeping the spacing between your lines even; crossing over some of the lines is OK. Use a matching thread for a subtle effect, or select a contrasting thread if you really want your quilting to stand out.

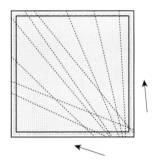

There's no need to stop with one set of radiating lines. Add as much texture as you'd like by continuing to add lines radiating from other corners. Rotate the quilt as needed so you always start stitching near the corner, working your way out across the quilt.

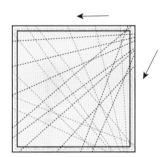

SHATTERED LINES

Similar to radiating lines, shattered lines create a linear texture by quilting across the surface of the quilt from one side to the other, although in a more random order. Start by marking and quilting a slightly angled line from one side of your practice piece to the other. Randomly quilt another angled straight line from one side to the other in another direction.

■ Detail of radiating lines on "Color Crystals" (page 34)

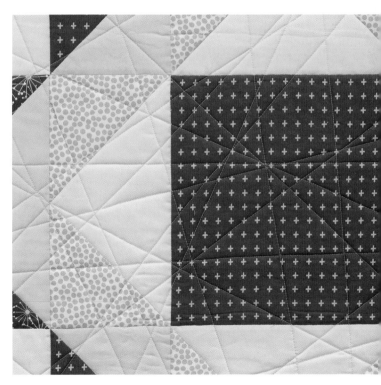

■ Detail of shattered lines on "Little Man's Fancy" (page 40)

■ Detail of walking-foot waves on "Static" (page 46)

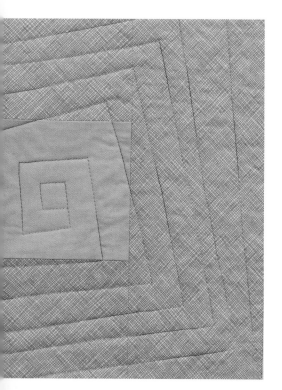

■ Detail of square spirals on "Square in a Square" (page 50)

Continue randomly adding horizontal and vertical lines across the surface of the quilt until it feels finished. My favorite method of marking this design is with a long piece of tape, repositioned and quilted one line at a time. This texture looks best when quilted with a thread that blends into most of the fabrics in your quilt top.

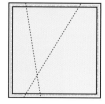 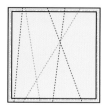 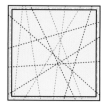

WALKING-FOOT WAVES

Gentle wavy lines can be quilted with your walking foot, adding organic texture in lieu of perfectly straight lines. Try substituting the straight lines of in-the-ditch quilting with waves instead. I like to call this "stitching *near* the ditch." You can combine horizontal waves with vertical waves to create a wavy grid like I did when quilting "Static." Walking-foot waves are easy to create by gently turning the quilt back and forth as you stitch, letting the machine do the work. The more often you move your quilt, the more waves you'll create.

As with straight-line quilting, always start at the top of your piece and work your way to the bottom. Divide your practice piece into four to five sections by eye. Quilt one wavy line in each section. If desired, you can place a piece of painter's tape to use as a guideline to keep your wiggly lines relatively parallel. Fill in the spaces by quilting additional wavy lines as desired. Rotate your practice piece 90° to quilt perpendicular waves, forming a wavy grid.

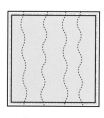 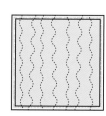 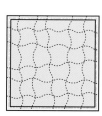

Loose waves   Tight waves   Wavy grid

SQUARE SPIRALS

Square spirals are fun to quilt on individual blocks and can be scaled up to quilt an entire quilt (similar to continuous spirals on page 20). They're time-consuming to do because they require turning the quilt a lot, but the geometric texture they create is striking. Good marking tools for this design are a ruler and washable marker or a hera. I use painter's tape, which requires stopping to remove the tape after each line is stitched and then repositioning the tape for the new line.

Refer to the illustration for the stitching path, beginning on any side of the practice piece. When you come to the edge of the piece, stop with your needle down in the fabric so the quilt doesn't shift, and then pivot and stitch the next line. You can complete as many rounds as you'd like. Rounds of stitching don't need to be spaced evenly or completely parallel to each other. When you get to the center of the block, pull your bobbin thread to the top and leave a tail to tie off later.

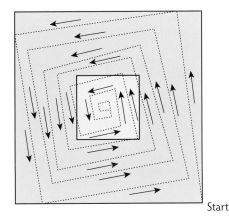

Start

The key difference between square spirals and continuous spirals is that square spirals start at the edge of a block or quilt and finish in the center. Continuous spirals start in the center and finish at the edge.

Starting and Ending a Line of Quilting

I try to quilt as much as I can without starting or stopping in the middle of the quilt, also known as "breaking thread." My favorite designs are those where I can start and end my stitching off an edge of the quilt, usually in the batting a couple of inches away from the edge of the quilt top. If the design calls for abrupt stops and starts, I'll use one of two methods, depending on my mood or the purpose of the quilt. For either method, bring the bobbin thread to the top by manually taking one stitch forward. Grasp the needle thread and pull the bobbin thread through with the point of your scissors or a hand-sewing needle. When you end a line of quilting, lift the foot and pull the quilt away from the machine to give the bobbin some slack. Cut both threads, leaving a tail. Gently tug on the needle thread until you see a loop of bobbin thread. Pull the thread through to the top.

UTILITARIAN METHOD. Bring both threads to the top of the quilt and start stitching with a series of six to eight tiny stitches to secure the stitching line. When you've finished the quilting, end with a series of six to eight tiny stitches, then bring the bobbin thread to the top and clip both threads close to the fabric.

SHOW-QUILT METHOD. Start by bringing both threads to the top of the quilt and stitch normally, leaving tails to tie off. When you finish stitching, leave ending tails as well. Then go back and tie a knot in each set of thread tails, using a self-threading needle to pop the knots into the batting.

If the thread breaks or you run out of bobbin, gently unpick enough stitches so you can bring up both threads and tie a knot to secure. Place your needle where you left off, bring up new threads, and continue quilting.

■ Detail of continuous spiral on "Focal Point" (page 58)

Easy ½" Measurement

On many machines, the distance from the needle to the outside edge of the walking foot is ½", or pretty close, perfect for quilting coninuous spirals.

CONTINUOUS SPIRAL

A continuous spiral starts at the center of a quilt and moves out to the edges. It adds incredible texture to a quilt and is actually easy to do; it's just time-consuming. The hardest part is starting the center, but once you get going, it can be applied to any quilt size!

1 Trace the 1½"-diameter circle pattern on page 21 onto template-making material and cut it out.

2 With a washable marker (that's been tested for removal), trace the circle onto the practice piece where you want the spiral to start.

3 Mark a line about ½" away from the center circle on the side opposite the point where you'll begin stitching.

4 Draw a line from the starting point, curving toward the midpoint of the line. Move the edge of your circle template as you draw to create a smooth, curving line. This will be the start of your spiral and no further marking is needed.

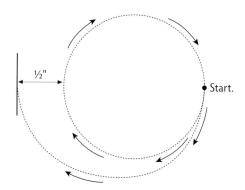

5 Once you're happy with your starting spiral shape, put the practice quilt sandwich under the machine and get ready to quilt. Move your needle position as needed or use a guide to give you a consistent ½" between stitching lines.

6 Bring the bobbin thread up to the surface of your quilt and hold both the top and bobbin thread as you make your first stitches.

7 Very slowly, quilt the outline of the circle, starting at the beginning of the marked spiral. If you have a knee lift for your machine, use it to lift the presser foot and rotate the quilt as you stitch.

8 Continue quilting the spiral and rotating the quilt as you go, pivoting as often as needed. Always stop stitching with the needle in the down position. Keep the edge of your walking foot right next to the previous line of stitching and sew slowly.

9 Continue quilting the spiral until you've reached the edge of the quilt and filled in all the spaces.

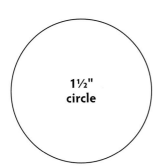

**1½"
circle**

Quilting Better Spirals

Practice the following tips to avoid spiraling out of control.

PICK YOUR DIRECTION. I quilted the spiral on "Focal Point" in a clockwise direction, keeping the right edge of my foot next to the previous line of quilting at all times. To quilt in a counterclockwise direction, keep the left edge of your foot next to the previous line of quilting.

LIFT AND ROTATE. For the first couple of rounds of the spiral, lift the presser foot and slightly rotate the quilt every two or three stitches. Quilt slowly for the first few rounds of spirals and be sure to take a break if you start to feel sore. It gets faster and easier as you go!

SPIRALING OFF THE EDGE. If the spiral doesn't stay on the quilt for the complete round, stitch a continuous line for as long as possible, and then go back and quilt additional echoing spiral lines to fill in any spaces in the quilt corners.

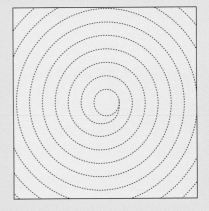

USE COMMON CENTS. Use a coin to change the diameter of the center circle.

RIPPLES

In this modernized version of a traditional Log Cabin design, the off-center blocks combined with decorative machine quilting look like water rippling across a pond.

Quilt Details

FINISHED QUILT: 66½" x 88½"

FINISHED BLOCK: 11" x 11"

DESIGN NOTES: Piles of scraps in two contrasting colors are sewn together around a center square to create 48 Wonky Log Cabin blocks set in a 6 x 8 grid. The blocks don't have equal numbers of strips on opposite sides of the center, and a few light blues mixed with a sprinkling of dark grays blurs the values, creating a bit of a transparency effect.

FABRIC: Gray and aqua scraps from my stash, plus fabrics from Robert Kaufman Fabrics, Riley Blake Designs, Andover Fabrics, and Moda

BATTING: Quilters Dream Cotton, Select loft, 100% cotton, white

QUILTING THREAD: Aurifil 50-weight cotton in Robin's Egg and Dove

MATERIALS

Yardage is based on 42"-wide fabric.

Approximately 5½ yards *total* of assorted gray scraps for blocks*

Approximately 5½ yards *total* of assorted blue and aqua scraps for blocks*

⅔ yard of gray print for binding

5½ yards of fabric for backing

72" x 93" piece of batting (twin size)

Approximately 800 yards *each* of light-gray and light-blue thread for machine quilting

12½" x 12½" square acrylic ruler

*Due to the improvisational nature of this quilt, the total amount of fabric you need may vary. The more fabrics you use, the better. Pieces should measure at least 1¼" wide and 12" long.

CUTTING

For faster cutting, stack up to four layers of fabric at once when you cut the gray, blue, and aqua strips for the blocks. Cut fewer strips to start, and then cut more as needed as you piece the blocks.

From the assorted gray scraps, cut:

Approximately 60 to 80 strips, 1¼" to 2½" wide x 42" long (or enough shorter strips, each at least 12" long, to total this amount). From the strips, crosscut 48 center pieces, approximately 2" to 2½" wide. Set aside the remainder of the strips for the block logs. Trim some of the center pieces so that one or more sides are at a slight angle.

From the assorted blue and aqua scraps, cut:

Approximately 60 to 80 strips, 1¼" to 2½" wide x 42" long (or enough shorter strips, each at least 12" long, to total this amount)

From the gray print for binding, cut:

9 strips, 2¼" x 42"

■ Designed, pieced, and quilted by Christa Watson

PIECING THE BLOCKS

Refer to "Helpful Hints" on page 25 before you begin sewing your blocks.

1 Sew a blue strip to one side of a gray center piece. Trim the strip ends even with the edges of the gray piece. If desired, slightly angle your ruler as you're trimming to give the block some wonkiness. Finger-press the seam allowances away from the center piece.

2 Using the remainder of the blue strip, sew the strip to another side of the gray piece that's adjacent to the previous blue side. Trim the strip ends even with the previous unit, again trimming at a slight angle if desired to add wonkiness. Finger-press the seam allowances away from the center piece.

3 Sew a gray strip to the remaining two sides of the center piece to complete the first round, trimming and pressing as before.

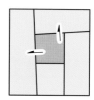

4 Select a different blue or aqua strip than you used for the first round. Working in the same manner as before, add the strip to the two adjacent sides on the blue half of the unit from step 3. Trim and press as before.

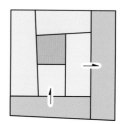

5 Select a different gray strip than you used for the first round. Add the strip to the two adjacent sides on the gray half of the previous unit. Trim and press as before to complete the second round.

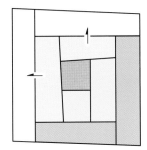

6 Continue adding rounds of strips in the established manner until the block measures larger than 11½" x 11½".

7 Repeat steps 1–6 to make a total of 48 blocks.

8 Press all of your blocks with an iron to set the seams and make them as flat as possible.

9 Using the 12½" square ruler, square up your blocks so they measure 11½" x 11½". If desired, turn the ruler so some of your blocks tilt slightly. To do this, lay the ruler on the block at the desired angle, making sure the 11½" line of the ruler has fabric under it on all sides. Trim along the right and top edges. Rotate the block 180° so the trimmed edges are on the left and bottom. Align the newly cut edges with the 11½" line of the ruler, and trim the right and top edges to square up the block.

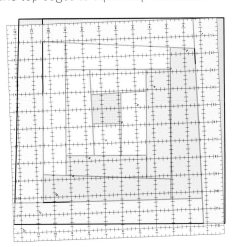

Helpful Hints

- To make the best use of your leftover strips, sew 8 to 12 blocks at a time. That way you can chain piece and use shorter leftover strips for the inner rounds when you start a new batch of blocks.

- It doesn't matter if you add your logs in a clockwise direction around the center piece or a counterclockwise direction, as long as roughly half of each block is blue/aqua and half is gray.

- A little wonkiness goes a long way; start with a slightly angled trim and add more angularity as desired once you see how it affects the shape of the block.

- Stack your strips next to your sewing machine in a few piles, keeping all of the same color together. Put shorter strips on top so they get used up first.

- Check your strip length before sewing each round of logs to make sure it's long enough; you may need to cut additional strips of the same fabric as you sew.

- If you have small leftover strips of the same fabric, you can piece them together to make a longer length if needed. This is supposed to be wonky, so random seams are OK!

- You don't have to use the same strip width for each round of logs; however, if your blocks begin to get too rectangular, compensate by adding narrower or wider strips as needed.

- Save some of the wider strips to use as your last round of logs because they may be trimmed the most.

ASSEMBLING THE QUILT TOP

1 Refer to the quilt assembly diagram below to lay out the blocks in eight rows of six blocks each.

2 Sew the blocks in each row together. Press the seam allowances open, or press them in alternating directions from row to row. Join the rows to complete the quilt top. Press the seam allowances open for a flatter quilt top or in the same direction for consistency.

3 Stitch ⅛" away from the edges on all four sides to prevent the edge seams from splitting open.

Quilt assembly

FINISHING

1 If you're using a single backing fabric, cut the yardage into two equal lengths and sew them together to make a backing that's approximately 6" longer and 6" wider than the quilt top.

2 Refer to "Layering and Basting" (page 106) to layer the quilt top, batting, and backing; baste the layers together using your preferred method.

3 Starting off of the quilt top at the upper-left corner as indicated in figure 1, use light-blue thread to quilt across the diagonal along the blue half of the blocks. When you get to the edge of the quilt, stop and turn your quilt to stitch along the blue half of the blocks in the bottom two rows, completing line 1 of your quilting. Stitch 1" or 2" beyond the quilt edge into the batting to secure your threads. Quilt lines 2–7 to secure the quilt layers, starting and stopping off the quilt each time. I call these "anchor lines." Rotate the quilt 180° degrees and quilt anchor lines 8–12, keeping the bulk of the quilt to your left as much as possible as you quilt.

4 Now that the quilt is anchored, you can quilt additional ripples in any section you like. I find it easiest to start on the right edge of the quilt and quilt sections 1–4, with the bulk of the quilt to my left. Rotate the quilt to finish quilting sections 5–7 (fig. 2).

FIG. 1

Variety Adds Spice

Change the spacing between the ripples and don't worry about keeping them perfectly parallel. The more lines of quilting you add, the less noticeable any mistakes and wobbles are!

5 Using light-gray thread, quilt ripples in the gray half of the blocks in the same manner. Quilt sections 1–3 first, and then rotate the quilt to finish sections 4–7 (fig. 3).

6 Refer to "Binding" (page 107) to bind the quilt edges by hand or machine using the gray print 2¼"-wide strips.

Pick a Stitch

The ripples quilting was done with a decorative stitch and a walking foot as explained on page 15. Choose an interesting stitch pattern that will add texture to your quilt, but that isn't too "thready." Adjust the stitch length and width if desired. If your machine only has straight-stitch capabilities, refer to "Walking-Foot Waves" (page 18) to create a similar look.

FIG. 2

FIG. 3

Quilting plan

RAIN

Pieced and quilted lines play nicely together in this minimalist design. My husband was doodling on his iPad one day and I thought his drawing would make a great quilt!

Quilt Details

FINISHED QUILT: 60" x 80"

DESIGN NOTES: Thin strips of color are pieced with large amounts of negative space to form a bold, graphic design that emphasizes lines. The strips are sewn parallel for easy construction, and the linear quilting, with its unexpected pops of color, adds an extra layer of texture to the composition.

FABRIC: Kona Cotton Solids by Robert Kaufman Fabrics in Rich Red, Curry, Grass Green, Denim, Pepper, and Snow

BATTING: Quilters Dream Cotton, Request loft, 100% cotton, white

QUILTING THREAD: Aurifil 50-weight cotton in Muslin; Aurifil 28-weight cotton in Red, Pale Yellow, Green Yellow, Blue Grey, and Medium Grey

MATERIALS

Yardage is based on 42"-wide fabric.*

5¼ yards of cream solid for background

⅞ yard of red solid for strips and binding

¼ yard of green solid for strips

¼ yard of black solid for strips

¼ yard of blue solid for strips

⅓ yard of yellow solid for strips

5 yards of fabric for backing

64" x 84" piece of batting

Approximately 700 yards of cream thread for machine quilting

Approximately 100 yards *each* of red, green, black, blue, and yellow thread to match strips for machine quilting

*For this quilt, I cut lengthwise strips (parallel to the selvage) for all of my pieces. To do the same requires 1¾ yards each of the solid colors. Cut as many pieces as needed to get the corresponding lengths listed in "Cutting the Rain Strips" (page 30) and "Cutting and Piecing the Background Strips" (page 31).

CUTTING THE RAIN STRIPS

To make piecing easier later, label each rain strip with the letter and number that follows the dimensions. For pieces longer than one strip length, join two strips end to end, and then crosscut it into the length needed, cutting as many of the shorter pieces as you can from the remainder of the strip.

From the cream solid, cut a *total* of:

17 strips, 2" x 42"; join the strips
    as needed and crosscut into:
      1 piece, 2" x 59½" (I2)
      1 piece, 2" x 42½" (H2)
      1 piece, 2" x 41½" (F2)
      1 piece, 2" x 40½" (M2)
      1 piece, 2" x 37" (E1)
      1 piece, 2" x 34" (J1)
      1 piece, 2" x 31" (G1)
      1 piece, 2" x 30" (L2)
      1 piece, 2" x 29" (N1)
      1 piece, 2" x 27" (H1)
      2 pieces, 2" x 26½" (B1, E2)
      1 piece, 2" x 21½" (K1)
      1 piece, 2" x 18" (D1)
      2 pieces, 2" x 16½" (D2, L1)
      1 piece, 2" x 15½" (F1)
      1 piece, 2" x 15" (A1)
      1 piece, 2" x 13" (C1)
      1 piece, 2" x 12½" (J2)
      1 piece, 2" x 11½" (A2)
      1 piece, 2" x 10½" (C2)
      2 pieces, 2" x 9½" (G2, I1)
      1 piece, 2" x 7½" (K2)
      1 piece, 2" x 5½" (B2)
      1 piece, 2" x 5" (M1)

From the red solid, cut:

3 strips, 2" x 42"; join the strips
    as needed and crosscut into:
      1 piece, 2" x 55½" (G)
      1 piece, 2" x 16" (M)
      1 piece, 2" x 12½" (A)
8 strips, 2¼" x 42"

From the green solid, cut:

3 strips, 2" x 42"; join the strips
    as needed and crosscut into:
      1 piece, 2" x 56½" (K)
      1 piece, 2" x 27" (H)
      1 piece, 2" x 18" (B)

From the black solid, cut:

3 strips, 2" x 42"; crosscut into:
      1 piece, 2" x 40" (C)
      1 piece, 2" x 30" (L)
      1 piece, 2" x 20" (E)

From the blue solid, cut:

3 strips, 2" x 42"; crosscut into:
      1 piece, 2" x 38" (D)
      1 piece, 2" x 27" (I)
      1 piece, 2" x 23½" (N)

From the yellow solid, cut:

4 strips, 2" x 42"; join the strips
    as needed and crosscut into:
      1 piece, 2" x 49½" (J)
      1 piece, 2" x 39½" (F)
      1 piece, 2" x 35½" (O)

Keep 'em Separated

This quilt is easier to assemble if you cut and piece the rain strips separately from the cream background strips.

PIECING THE RAIN STRIPS

With the exception of N and O, assemble the strips by sewing cream strips to each end of the colored strip of the same letter. Pieces labeled with a *1* are sewn to the left end of the colored strips and pieces labeled *2* are sewn to the right end. For blue piece N, sew cream piece N1 to the left end of the piece. Yellow piece O is not pieced. Press all of the seam allowances open.

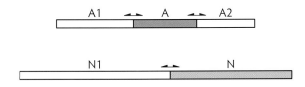

CUTTING AND PIECING THE BACKGROUND STRIPS

To make piecing easier later, label each cream background strip with the number that follows the dimensions. For pieces longer than one strip length, join the number of strips needed end to end to achieve the required length, and then crosscut the pieced strip into the length needed, cutting as many shorter pieces as you can from the remainder of the strip.

From the remainder of the cream solid, cut:

2 strips, 6" x 42"; join the strips and trim to make:
 1 piece, 6" x 48" (17)
2 strips, 5½" x 42"; crosscut into:
 1 piece, 5½" x 24½" (2)
 1 piece, 5½" x 12" (1)
 1 piece, 5½" x 11½" (20)
5 strips, 5" x 42"; join the strips and crosscut into:
 1 piece, 5" x 94½" (8)
 1 piece, 5" x 72" (15)

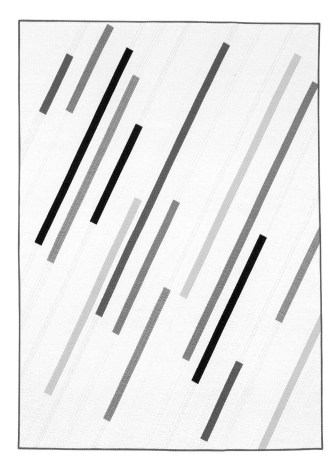

■ Designed, pieced, and quilted by Christa Watson

9 strips, 4½" x 42"; join the strips and crosscut into:
 1 piece, 4½" x 96½" (11)
 1 piece, 4½" x 94½" (13)
 1 piece, 4½" x 59½" (5)
 1 piece, 4½" x 34½" (3)
 1 piece, 4½" x 31" (18)
 1 piece, 4½" x 21" (19)
6 strips, 3½" x 42"; join the strips and crosscut into:
 1 piece, 3½" x 96½" (10)
 1 piece, 3½" x 79" (7)
 1 piece, 3½" x 46" (4)
8 strips, 2½" x 42"; join the strips and crosscut into:
 1 piece, 2½" x 95½" (12)
 1 piece, 2½" x 80½" (14)
 1 piece, 2½" x 68½" (6)
 1 piece, 2½" x 57½" (16)
3 strips, 1½" x 42"; join the strips and trim to make
 1 piece, 1½" x 95" (9)

ASSEMBLING THE QUILT TOP

1 Lay out the rain strips and background strips diagonally in the order shown. Stagger the strips so they line up similarly to the diagram, but don't worry about being exact; extra fabric has been added to the ends of each strip to account for slight inconsistencies, and a little variation is OK.

2 Join the strips in pairs, sewing each pair in the same direction. Press the seam allowances open. Join the pairs, sewing in the opposite direction than before to prevent the strips from bowing. Press the seam allowances open. The staggered edges of the quilt top will be trimmed later.

Stack and Snap

For faster assembly, pair strips right sides together as you remove them from your design area, and then stack the strips in order next to your machine. Take a picture with your camera phone or other device to refer to as you assemble the strips.

Squaring Up

Lay out your quilt top on a large, flat surface. With a straight edge and a 90° corner square, mark the boundary with a water-soluble pen. Cut on the lines.

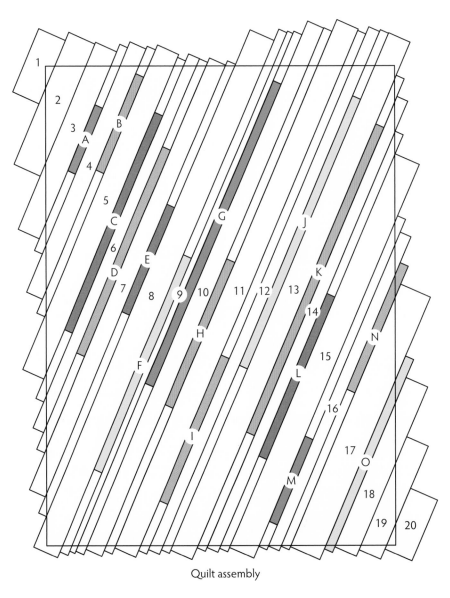

Quilt assembly

3 Square up the quilt top to 60" x 80". Or, if you prefer, quilt first and trim later.

4 Stitch ⅛" from the edges on all four sides to prevent the edge seams from splitting open.

FINISHING

1 Cut the backing yardage into two equal lengths and sew them together to make a backing approximately 6" longer and 6" wider than the quilt top.

2 Refer to "Layering and Basting" (page 106) to layer the quilt top, batting, and backing; baste the layers together using your preferred method.

3 Using a walking foot and cream thread, stitch in the ditch along each diagonal seam to anchor the quilt. You may wish to skip a few of these anchor lines and quilt them later with colored thread. You can either stitch in the ditch across the quilt from right to left, rotating the quilt as needed, or quilt the longest diagonal first and work your way across each half of the quilt as desired. Be sure to start and end your lines of stitching off the quilt, avoiding the need to bury your thread tails.

4 Quilt parallel lines (see page 15) on the background strips between each of the pieced rain strips, working from the side to the center of the quilt, and then rotating and working from the center to the side as before. Use the seam lines and the edge of the walking foot as guides to stitch the lines, changing the needle position as desired to vary the spacing in between. Don't worry about keeping your lines perfectly straight; aim for texture over perfection.

■ Stitch in the ditch to anchor the quilt. Then quilt the background strips, and finally, the rain strips.

5 Quilt parallel lines on the rain strips, changing thread color to match the color of each strip.

Timesaving Tip

For efficiency, quilt all strips of the same color before switching threads.

6 Refer to "Binding" (page 107) to bind the quilt edges by hand or machine using the red 2¼"-wide strips.

COLOR CRYSTALS

A bold combination of line and color, this quilt is made from just two rolls of precut strips. Leftover strips are combined with an extra bit of background to form a secondary composition on the back (page 39), and the simplicity of the design allows you to get to the quilting quickly!

Quilt Details

FINISHED QUILT: 54½" x 62½"

DESIGN NOTES: This quilt is made from 31 rows that each finish 2" wide. The strips are sewn into three sections which are then joined to make the top. The stair-step intervals in each section increase or decrease by 4". The linear quilting adds an extra layer of depth to the design.

FABRIC: Kona Cotton Solids Roll Ups by Robert Kaufman Fabrics in Kona Black and New Bright, plus black solid yardage

BATTING: Hobbs Heirloom, 80% cotton/20% polyester, black

QUILTING THREAD: Aurifil 50-weight cotton in Black, Variegated French Lilac, Variegated Limoni di Monterosso, and Variegated Creme de Menthe

MATERIALS

Yardage is based on 42"-wide fabric.

40 black-solid precut 2½" x 42" strips for front and binding*
40 assorted bright-solid precut 2½" x 42" strips for front and backing**
1¾ yards of black solid for pieced backing**
59" x 67" piece of black batting
Approximately 400 yards of black thread for machine quilting
Approximately 150 yards *each* of variegated teal thread, variegated pink-and-purple thread, and variegated yellow-and-orange thread for machine quilting

If you want to cut your own 2½"-wide strips, you'll need approximately 3 yards.

**If you don't want to piece your backing from the leftover 2½" strips, you'll need a total of 27 bright precut strips for the front and 3¾ yards of fabric for the back.*

CHOOSING AND CUTTING THE STRIPS

1 From the assorted bright precut strips, select nine strips ranging from blue to green for section A, nine strips ranging from pink to purple for section B, and nine strips ranging from red to yellow for section C. Set aside the remaining strips for the backing.

2 Referring to the photo (page 36) if needed, lay out the colored strips selected for section A in the desired order from top to bottom. Number the strips from 1 to 9, with 1 at the top and 9 at the bottom. Cut the strips into the following lengths:

    Strips 1 and 9: 12½"
    Strips 2 and 8: 16½"
    Strips 3 and 7: 20½"
    Strips 4 and 6: 24½"
    Strip 5: 28½"

■ Designed, pieced, and quilted by Christa Watson

3 Cut the black strips into lengths as follows for section A, piecing strips as needed to achieve the required length.

 Strips 1 and 9: 42½"
 Strips 2 and 8: 38½"
 Strips 3 and 7: 34½"
 Strips 4 and 6: 30½"
 Strip 5: 26½"

4 Repeat steps 2 and 3 to cut strips for sections B and C.

5 Piece and trim additional precut black strips to make four strips that measure 54½".

Cutting Long Strips

To cut strips that are longer than your cutting mat or ruler, fold them in half and trim off the selvages. Measure from the fold half the distance needed and make the cut. For instance, for the 42½"-long strip, measure and cut 21¼" from the fold.

ASSEMBLING THE SECTIONS

1 Using the bright and black strips for section A, sew each bright strip to the end of the appropriate-length black strip as shown to make strips measuring 54½" long. Press the seam allowances open.

2 Sew the pieced strips together along the long edges in numerical order. Press the seam allowances open.

1	2½" x 12½"	2½" x 42½"
2	2½" x 16½"	2½" x 38½"
3	2½" x 20½"	2½" x 34½"
4	2½" x 24½"	2½" x 30½"
5	2½" x 28½"	2½" x 26½"
6	2½" x 24½"	2½" x 30½"
7	2½" x 20½"	2½" x 34½"
8	2½" x 16½"	2½" x 38½"
9	2½" x 12½"	2½" x 42½"

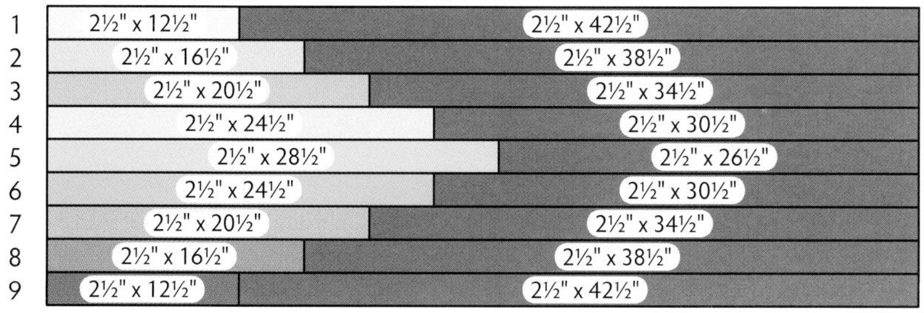

3 Repeat steps 1 and 2 with the section B and C pieces to complete sections B and C.

ASSEMBLING THE QUILT TOP

1 Refer to the quilt assembly diagram to lay out sections A–C and the pieced black 54½"-long strips as shown. Sew the strips and sections together. Press the seam allowances open.

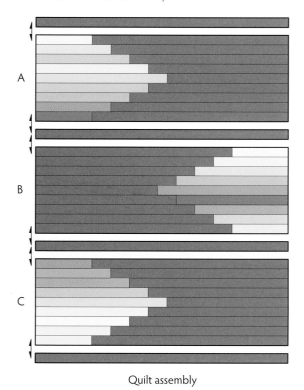

Quilt assembly

Going in Different Directions

To keep the long strips from warping or bowing, alternate the direction you sew each time you add a strip.

COLOR CRYSTALS

2 Stitch ⅛" from the edges on all four sides to prevent the edge seams from splitting open.

FINISHING

1 Refer to "Technicolor Backing" (page 39) to piece the backing from the leftover bright and black precut strips, plus yardage. Or, if you're making the backing from a single piece of fabric, cut the yardage into two equal lengths and sew them together to make a backing approximately 6" longer and 6" wider than the quilt top.

2 Refer to "Layering and Basting" (page 106) to layer the quilt top, batting, and backing; baste the layers together using your preferred method.

3 Referring to the quilting plan, right, use black thread and your walking foot to stitch in the ditch around each of the three color sections to anchor the quilt. Pivot the quilt as needed while quilting.

4 Using your preferred marking method (I used a hera marker and a long ruler), mark a series of straight lines radiating from the top-right corner of the quilt. Use more than one ruler as needed to span the length of the desired line, or carefully slide your ruler as you go to create a long enough line.

5 Quilt the marked lines, starting from either the edge of the quilt and working to the end of the line, or from the middle of the quilt to the edge—whichever way is easier to slide the quilt through the machine. Pull your bobbin thread up to the top when starting or ending a line of stitching in the middle of the quilt; tie off the threads when you finish quilting all the lines.

Crossing Paths

Your lines don't need to be perfectly spaced, nor do they need to emanate from the same spot. Some of them can even cross. The more variety the better!

6 Repeat steps 4 and 5 to mark and quilt the lines radiating from the bottom-right corner of the quilt. Refer to page 17 for more tips on quilting radiating lines.

7 Remove the walking foot and attach a free-motion foot. Use a variegated thread that blends with all of the color sections or change the thread to match each color section.

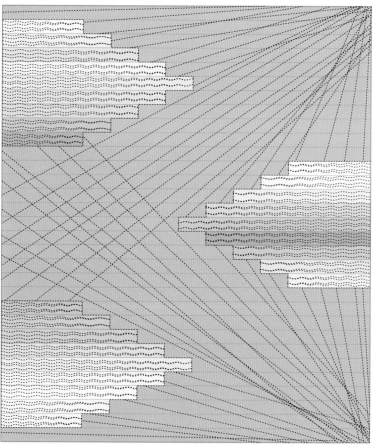

Quilt plan

8 Refer to page 66 to free-motion quilt "Seaweed" in each color section. Starting and stopping off of the quilt, stitch to the end of a strip, heading toward the center of the quilt. Pause briefly to bring the free-motion foot back toward the edge of the quilt. Quilt each strip in each section in the same manner, completing an entire color section in the same sitting if possible to maintain consistency.

Design Options

If you're not yet comfortable with free-motion quilting, the color sections can be quilted with your walking foot using a gentle turning motion (see "Walking-Foot Waves" on page 18).

9 Refer to "Binding" (page 107) to bind the quilt edges by hand or machine using the black precut strips. Because the strips are slightly wider than normal, you may want to use a slightly wider seam allowance to attach the binding to the quilt.

Technicolor Backing

Use up leftover strips to create a colorful mosaic. Float your design in the middle of the quilt like I did, or add additional sections for a completely scrappy quilt back. The backing finishes to approximately 60" x 70".

MATERIALS

Yardage is based on 42"-wide fabric.

28 precut bright-colored 2½" x 42" strips*, *OR* leftovers to total this much

1⅛ yards of black solid

*If you want to cut your own 2½"-wide strips, you'll need approximately 2⅛ yards total of assorted fabrics. Strips will be pieced together, so they don't need to be the full 42" length of a precut strip.

CUTTING

From the *lengthwise* grain of the black solid, cut:

2 strips, 17½" x 60"

MAKING THE BACKING

1. Randomly cut the bright 2½" x 42" strips into two to four shorter lengths.

2. Join the bright strips end to end to make 18 pieced strips measuring 60" long, trimming the strips as needed to achieve the correct length.

3. Sew the strips together along the long edges, sewing pairs of strips together first, and then sewing the pairs together. Press the seam allowances open.

4. Join a black 17½" x 60" strip to the top and bottom edge of the pieced bright panel along the long edges. Press the seam allowances open.

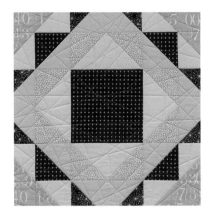

LITTLE MAN'S FANCY

I love single, jumbo-block quilts, especially for baby-shower gifts. They go together quickly and make great practice quilts for machine quilting.

Quilt Details

FINISHED QUILT: 36½" x 36½"

FINISHED BLOCK: 12" x 12"

DESIGN NOTES: A traditional block called Gentleman's Fancy inspired me to make this quilt. By changing the color placement, rotating a few lines, and supersizing the block, I created a new look from an old favorite. Make the quilt monochromatic like I did, or change up the colors for even more variety.

FABRIC: Figures by Zen Chic and Bella Solids, both by Moda

BATTING: Quilters Dream Cotton, Deluxe loft, 100% cotton, natural

QUILTING THREAD: Aurifil 50-weight cotton in Robin's Egg

MATERIALS

Yardage is based on 42"-wide fabric. Fat quarters measure approximately 18" x 21".

½ yard of light-blue solid for block backgrounds

½ yard of light-gray solid for block backgrounds

½ yard of medium-blue numbers print for Double Half-Square-Triangle blocks

½ yard of dark-blue plus-sign print for center block and Double Half-Square-Triangle blocks

1 fat quarter of medium-blue dot print for Double Flying Geese blocks

1 fat quarter of dark-blue fireworks print for Double Flying Geese blocks

⅜ yard of navy solid for binding

1⅓ yards of fabric for backing

41" x 41" piece of batting

Approximately 200 yards of blue thread that blends with the fabrics for machine quilting

CUTTING

Cut strips from the lengthwise grain (parallel to the selvage) unless otherwise noted. Keep pieces cut from the same fabric together to prevent mix-ups when piecing the blocks.

From the light-blue solid, cut:
2 strips, 6⅞" x 18"; crosscut into 4 squares, 6⅞" x 6⅞". Cut each square in half diagonally to make 8 triangles.
1 square, 13¼" x 13¼"

From the light-gray solid, cut:
1 strip, 6⅞" x 18"; crosscut into 2 squares, 6⅞" x 6⅞"
1 square, 13¼" x 13¼"

Continued on page 42

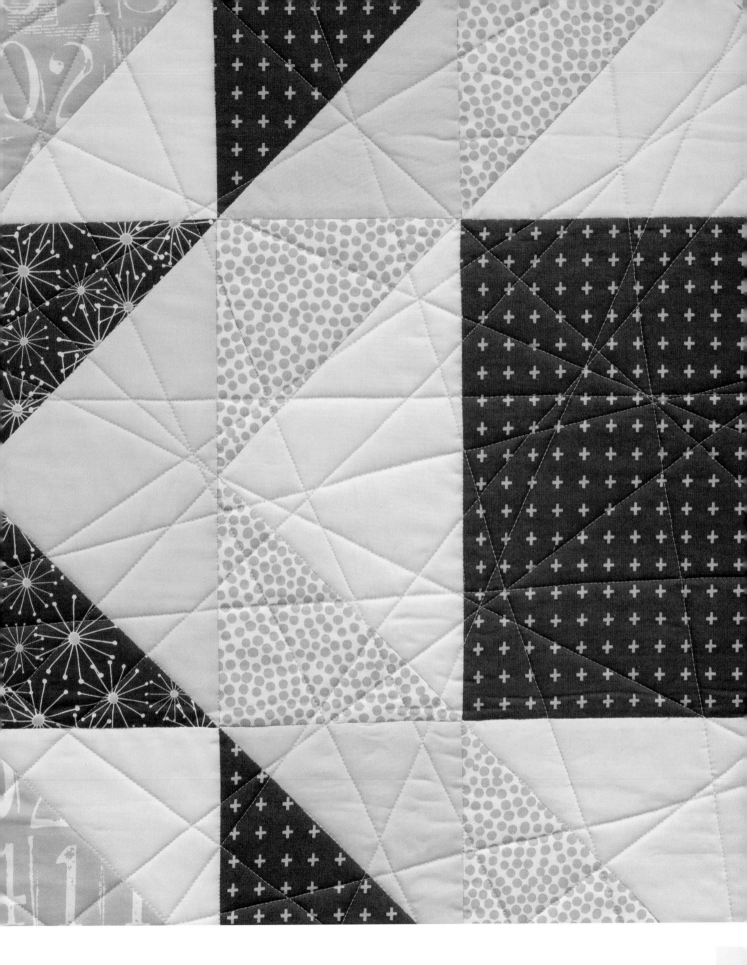

Continued from page 40

From the medium-blue dot print, cut:

2 strips, 6⅞" x 18"; crosscut into 4 squares, 6⅞" x 6⅞"

From the medium-blue numbers print, cut:

2 strips, 12⅞" x 18"; crosscut into 2 squares, 12⅞" x 12⅞". Cut each square in half diagonally to make four triangles. If you're using a directional print, cut one square from bottom left to top right and the remaining square from bottom right to top left to create four large triangles with the print going in the same direction on the finished quilt.

From the dark-blue plus-sign print, cut:

1 strip, 6⅞" x 18"; crosscut into 2 squares, 6⅞" x 6⅞"
1 square, 12½" x 12½"

From the dark-blue fireworks print, cut:

2 strips, 6⅞" x 18"; crosscut into 4 squares, 6⅞" x 6⅞"

From the *crosswise grain* of the navy solid, cut:

4 strips, 2¼" x 42"

PIECING THE DOUBLE FLYING GEESE BLOCKS

If you're working with directional prints, refer to "Working with Directional Prints" (page 61) to orient the pieces so they run the desired direction in the finished pieces.

1 Place two medium-blue dot 6⅞" squares on opposite corners of the light-blue solid 13¼" square as shown, right sides together. The smaller squares will overlap slightly. Draw a diagonal line from corner to corner across the dot squares. Pin them in place to keep them from shifting.

Sew ¼" from both sides of the marked line. Cut the pieces apart on the marked line. Press the seam allowances open.

2 Place one of the remaining medium-blue dot 6⅞" squares on the corner of the larger triangle of a unit from step 1, right sides together. Mark a diagonal line on the dot square as shown. Stitch ¼" from both sides of the marked line, and then cut the pieces apart on the marked line to make two flying-geese units. Press the seam allowances open and trim the dog-eared triangle tips. Repeat with the remaining unit from step 1 to make a total of four medium-blue flying-geese units.

Make 4.

3 Repeat steps 1 and 2 using the dark-blue fireworks 6⅞" squares and light-gray solid 13¼" square to make a total of four dark-blue flying-geese units.

4 Join each medium-blue flying geese unit to a dark-blue flying-geese unit as shown to create four Double Flying Geese blocks. Press the seam allowances open.

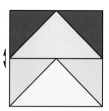

Make 4.

PIECING THE DOUBLE HALF-SQUARE-TRIANGLE BLOCKS

1 Layer each light-gray solid 6⅞" square over a dark-blue plus-sign print 6⅞" square. Draw a diagonal line from corner to corner on the wrong side of each light-gray square. Sew ¼" from both sides of the marked line. Cut the squares apart on the marked lines to make a total of four half-square-triangle units. Press the seam allowances open. Trim the units to 6½" square if needed.

Make 4.

2 Sew a light-blue solid triangle to adjacent sides of each half-square-triangle unit from step 1. Press the seam allowances open.

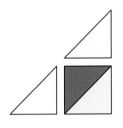 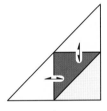

Make 4.

3 Join a medium-blue numbers print triangle to each unit from step 2. Be sure to orient the print correctly if using a directional print. Press the seam allowances open.

Make 4.

■ Designed, pieced, and quilted by Christa Watson

Triangle Tip Placement

When working with triangles, use a single-hole needle plate, also known as a straight-stitch plate and sew with the straight edge under the needle and the triangle tip pointing toward you (as in step 2 at left). This will prevent the tips from being sucked into the machine.

When sewing triangles like those in step 2, match the short side of the triangle with the edge of the square so that the triangle tip extends beyond the edge of the square.

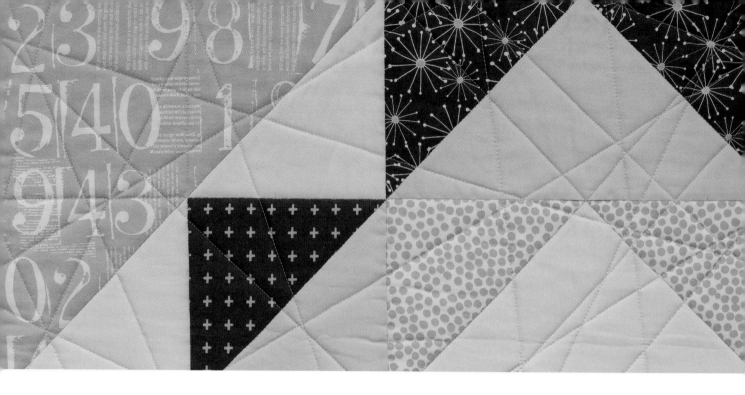

ASSEMBLING THE QUILT TOP

1 Refer to the quilt assembly diagram to lay out the blocks and dark-blue plus-sign 12½" square into three rows. Join the blocks in each row. Press the seam allowances open. Join the rows. Press the seam allowances open.

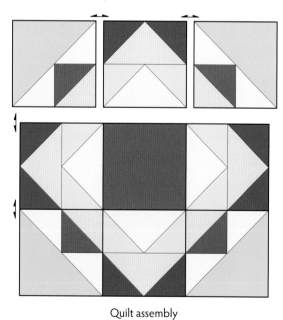

Quilt assembly

2 Stitch ⅛" from the edges on all four sides to prevent the edge seams from splitting open.

Change It Up

By flipping the direction of the Double Flying Geese blocks, you can create a whole new look. Just imagine how pretty this would look in pink for a baby girl!

FINISHING

1 Refer to "Layering and Basting" (page 106) to layer the quilt top, batting, and backing; baste the layers together using your preferred method.

2 Using a walking foot and the blue thread, stitch in the ditch of the block joining seams first, and then stitch the diagonal seams running along the dark-blue half-square triangles. This will anchor the piece for additional quilting.

3 Refer to "Shattered Lines" (page 17) to mark and stitch random straight lines from one edge of the quilt to the other, starting and ending off the quilt.

4 Refer to "Binding" (page 107) to bind the quilt edges by hand or machine using the navy 2¼"-wide strips.

Quilting plan

STATIC

Create a colorful quilt from pixelated patchwork. Strip piecing makes quick work of this scrappy beauty.

Quilt Details

FINISHED QUILT: 56½" x 64½"

FINISHED BLOCK: 8" x 8"

DESIGN NOTES: This random-looking design is created from 56 of the same "pixel" blocks rotated in different positions and set together in a 7 x 8 grid. I chose 16 fabrics in a palette of pink, purple, and yellow and quilted a subtle design with blending threads, but you can opt for a super-scrappy quilt made from precut strips or scraps. Contain the chaos with a simple frame of solid-colored binding.

FABRIC: True Colors from FreeSpirit Fabric

BATTING: Hobbs Tuscany Wool, 100% wool, natural

QUILTING THREAD: An assortment of 40- and 50-weight Aurifil cottons in shades of yellow, pink, and purple

MATERIALS

Yardage is based on 42"-wide fabric.

⅜ yard *each* of 16 assorted prints for blocks
⅝ yard of coordinating solid fabric for binding
3⅞ yards of fabric for backing
61" x 69" piece of batting
Approximately 500 yards of thread for machine quilting

CUTTING

From *each* of the 16 assorted prints, cut:
4 strips, 2½" x 42" (64 total)

From the coordinating solid, cut:
7 strips, 2¼" x 42"

PIECING THE BLOCKS

1 Separate the strips by print, and then label them 1–16.

2 Join one strip *each* of fabrics 1–4 along the long edges in numerical order to make strip set A, sewing the seams in opposite directions to keep the strips from bowing. Repeat to make a total of four strip sets. Press the seam allowances open. Crosscut the strip sets into 56 A segments, 2½" wide.

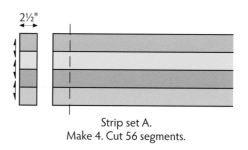

2½"

Strip set A.
Make 4. Cut 56 segments.

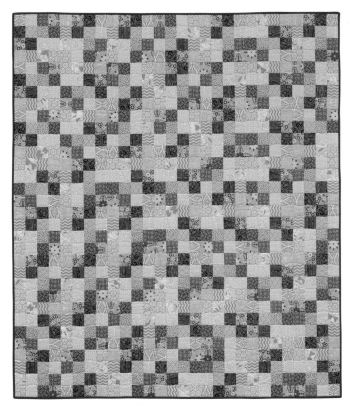

■ Designed, pieced, and quilted by Christa Watson

Strip-Set Tips

- Shorten your stitch length when sewing the strips together. This will help keep the seams from coming apart when the strip sets are cut apart.

- Sew strips 1 and 2 together with fabric 2 on top. Sew strips 3 and 4 together with fabric 4 on top. Join strips 1-2 with strips 3-4, sewing with fabric 2 on top. This will automatically reverse the sewing direction for you. Use this technique with each set of strips.

- For ease in opening the seams for pressing, cut the strip sets in half.

- Cut carefully so that you get at least 14 segments per strip set.

3 Repeat step 1 with fabrics 5–8 to make 56 B segments.

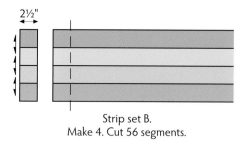

Strip set B.
Make 4. Cut 56 segments.

4 Repeat step 1 with fabrics 9–12 to make 56 C segments.

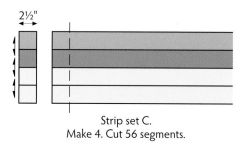

Strip set C.
Make 4. Cut 56 segments.

5 Repeat step 1 with fabrics 13–16 to make 56 D segments.

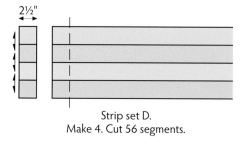

Strip set D.
Make 4. Cut 56 segments.

6 Working in alphabetical order, join one each of segments A–D to make a block. Repeat to make a total of 56 blocks. Press the seam allowances open.

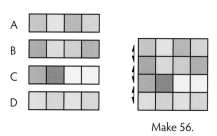

Make 56.

ASSEMBLING THE QUILT TOP

1 Refer to the quilt assembly diagram below to lay out the blocks in eight rows of seven blocks each, rotating the blocks as desired to create a pixelated effect. It's alright if the same fabrics touch! Sew the blocks in each row together. Press the seam allowances open. Join the rows. Press the seam allowances open (fig. 1).

2 Stitch ⅛" from the edges on all four sides to prevent the edge seams from splitting open.

FINISHING

1 Cut the backing fabric into two equal lengths; sew them together to make a backing approximately 6" longer and 6" wider than the quilt top.

2 Refer to "Layering and Basting" (page 106) to layer the quilt top, batting, and backing; baste the layers together using your preferred method.

3 Using a walking foot and a thread color that blends with the quilt-top fabrics, and referring to the quilting plan below, start on one side of the quilt and stitch walking-foot waves (see page 18) every four squares across the quilt to anchor the layers. Start and end the lines of stitching off the quilt so you don't have to bury the threads in the quilt. Work from the side toward the quilt center, and then rotate the quilt 180° and begin quilting where you left off at the center and work toward the other side. Rotate the quilt 90° and repeat to quilt wavy lines perpendicular to the first set of lines (fig. 2).

4 Add additional lines of wavy quilting between all of the vertical and horizontal rows as desired.

5 Refer to "Binding" (page 107) to bind the quilt edges by hand or machine using the coordinating solid 2¼"-wide strips.

FIG. 1

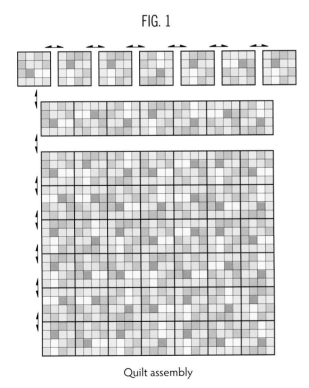

Quilt assembly

FIG. 2

Quilting plan

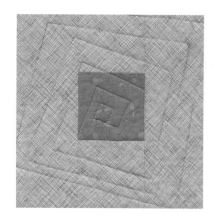

SQUARE IN A SQUARE

With plenty of wide-open spaces to practice your quilting, this simple yet striking design sews together quickly. The name is a play on the traditional Square-in-a-Square block, interpreted here in a fresh, new way.

Quilt Details

FINISHED QUILT: 60½" x 60½"

FINISHED BLOCKS: 12" x 12", 9" x 9", and 6" x 6"

DESIGN NOTES: Fourteen square blocks, combined with background rectangles, are then sewn into panels to form the final square design. All three sizes of blocks are pieced in the same manner. If you'd like to make a larger quilt, sew more blocks and add additional panels as needed.

FABRIC: Botanics by Carolyn Friedlander and coordinating Kona Cotton Solids in Silver (background) and Blue Celestial (binding), all by Robert Kaufman Fabrics

BATTING: Hobbs Tuscany Silk, 90% silk/10% polyester, natural

QUILTING THREAD: Aurifil Cotton 40-weight in Dove and 50-weight in Marrakesh

MATERIALS

Yardage is based on 42"-wide fabric. Fat eighths measure approximately 9" x 21".

2⅔ yards of light-gray solid for background

¼ yard *each* of 7 assorted medium- to dark-value fabrics for large blocks

1 fat eighth *each* of 7 assorted medium- to dark-value fabrics for small and medium blocks

⅝ yard of dark-blue solid for binding

4 yards of fabric for backing

65" x 65" piece of batting

Approximately 200 yards of variegated thread for machine quilting the blocks

Approximately 600 yards of light-gray thread for machine quilting the background

CUTTING

From *each* of the 7 assorted quarter-yard cuts, cut:
1 strip, 4½" x 42"; crosscut into:
    2 rectangles, 4½" x 12½" (14 total)
    3 squares, 4½" x 4½" (21 total)

From *each* of 4 of the assorted fat eighths, cut:
2 strips, 3½" x 21"; crosscut into:
    2 rectangles, 3½" x 9½" (8 total)
    3 squares, 3½" x 3½" (12 total)

From *each of the 3* remaining assorted fat eighths, cut:
2 strips, 2½" x 21"; crosscut into:
    2 rectangles, 2½" x 6½" (6 total)
    3 squares, 2½" x 2½" (9 total)

Continued on page 52

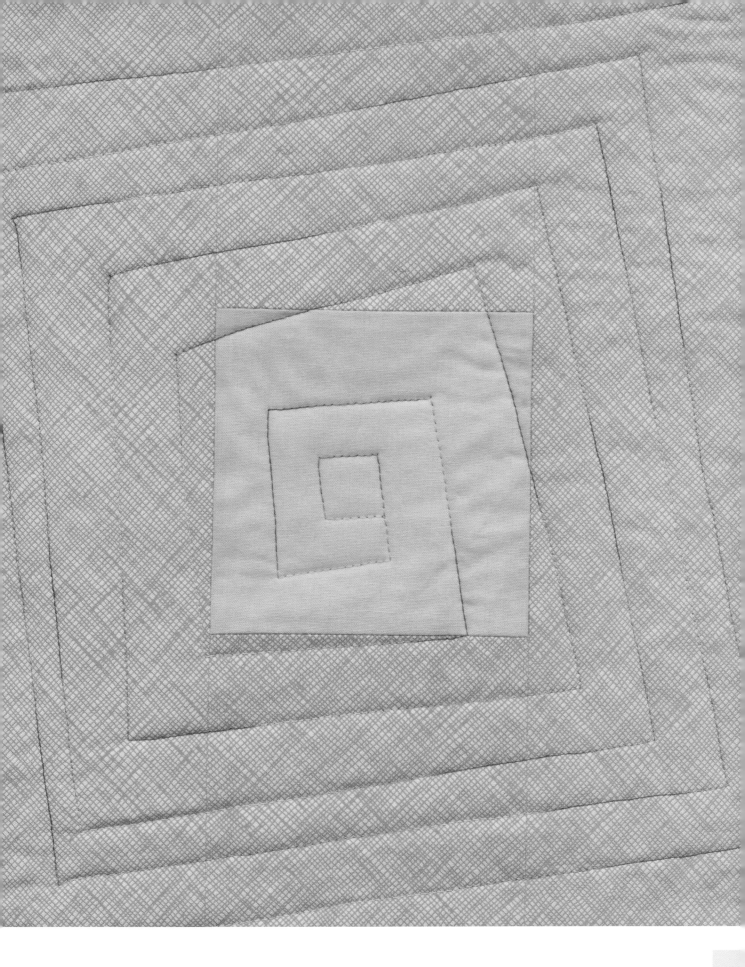

■ Designed, pieced, and quilted by Christa Watson

Stay Organized

Label each gray rectangle with a small piece of painter's tape; write the size on the tape. Place the tape in the center of each piece and leave it in place until the quilt top is sewn together.

Continued from page 50

From the light-gray solid, cut:

1 strip, 9½" x 42"; crosscut into
  2 rectangles, 9½" x 12½"
1 strip, 8½" x 42"; crosscut into
  1 rectangle, 8½" x 15½"
1 strip, 7½" x 42"; crosscut into:
  1 rectangle, 7½" x 20½"
  1 rectangle, 7½" x 12½"
4 strips, 6½" x 42"; crosscut into:
  1 rectangle, 6½" x 20½"
  1 rectangle, 6½" x 16½"
  2 rectangles, 6½" x 15½"
  2 rectangles, 6½" x 13½"
  2 rectangles, 6½" x 9½"
  3 rectangles, 6½" x 7½"
2 strips, 5½" x 42"; crosscut into:
  1 rectangle, 5½" x 12½"
  2 rectangles, 5½" x 11½"
  1 rectangle, 5½" x 9½"
3 strips, 4½" x 42"; crosscut into:
  1 rectangle, 4½" x 20½"
  1 rectangle, 4½" x 16½"
  4 rectangles, 4½" x 12½"
2 strips, 3½" x 42"; crosscut into:
  1 rectangle, 3½" x 19½"
  1 rectangle, 3½" x 13½"
  1 rectangle, 3½" x 12½"
  1 rectangle, 3½" x 9½"
  1 rectangle, 3½" x 6½"
1 strip, 2½" x 42"; crosscut into:
  1 rectangle, 2½" x 13½"
  1 rectangle, 2½" x 9½"
  1 rectangle, 2½" x 6½"
1 strip, 1½" x 42"; crosscut into:
  1 rectangle, 1½" x 12½"
  2 rectangles, 1½" x 9½"

From the dark-blue solid, cut:

7 strips, 2¼" x 42"

PIECING THE BLOCKS

1 Select a 4½" square from one medium to dark fabric. From a different medium to dark fabric, select two 4½" squares and two 4½" x 12½" rectangles. Sew the matching squares to opposite sides of the remaining square. Press the seam allowances open. Join the rectangles to the long edges of the unit. Press the seam allowances open. Repeat to make a total of seven large blocks.

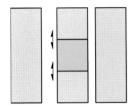 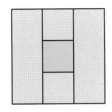

Large block.
Make 7.

2 Referring to step 1 and using a 3½" square from one fabric and two 3½" squares and two 3½" x 9½" rectangles from a different fabric, make a medium block. Repeat to make a total of four medium blocks.

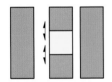

Medium block.
Make 4.

3 Referring to step 1 and using a 2½" square from one fabric and two 2½" squares and two 2½" x 6½" rectangles from a different fabric, make a small block. Repeat to make a total of three small blocks.

Small block.
Make 3.

ASSEMBLING THE QUILT TOP

1 Lay out two large blocks, one medium block, and the light-gray rectangles indicated into three sections as shown. Sew the pieces in each section together. Press the seam allowances open.

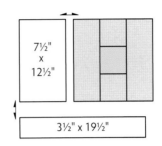

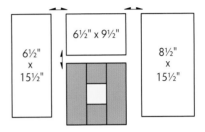

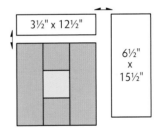

2 Sew the step 1 sections together to make panel A. Press the seam allowances open.

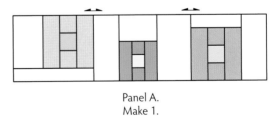

Panel A.
Make 1.

3 Lay out two large blocks, one small block, and the light-gray rectangles indicated into three sections as shown. Sew the pieces in each section together. Press the seam allowances open.

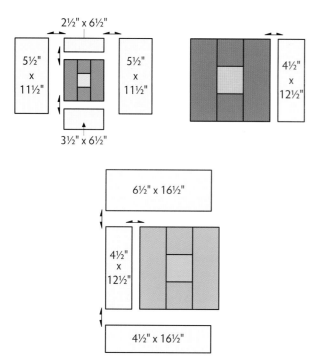

2½" x 6½"

5½" x 11½"

5½" x 11½"

3½" x 6½"

4½" x 12½"

6½" x 16½"

4½" x 12½"

4½" x 16½"

4 Sew the step 3 sections together to make panel B. Press the seam allowances open.

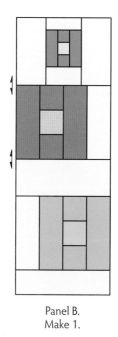

Panel B.
Make 1.

5 Lay out one large block, one medium block, one small block, and the light-gray rectangles indicated into three sections as shown. Sew the pieces in each section together. Press the seam allowances open.

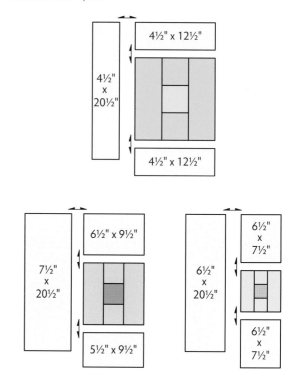

4½" x 12½"

4½" x 20½"

4½" x 12½"

6½" x 9½"

6½" x 7½"

7½" x 20½"

6½" x 20½"

5½" x 9½"

6½" x 7½"

6 Join the step 5 sections as before to make panel C. Press the seam allowances open.

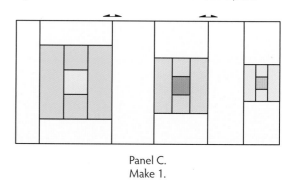

Panel C.
Make 1.

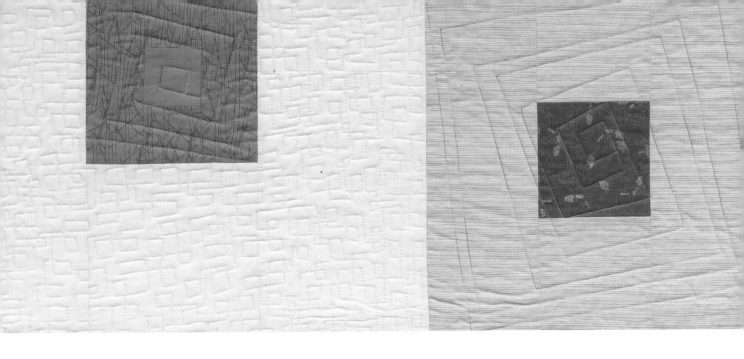

7 Repeat step 5 with the pieces shown to make three sections as shown.

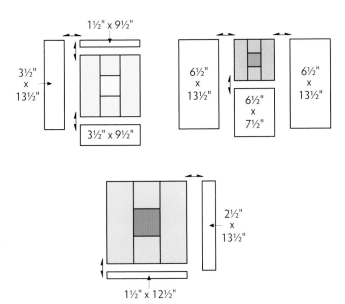

1½" x 9½"

3½"
x
13½"

3½" x 9½"

6½"
x
13½"

6½"
x
7½"

6½"
x
13½"

2½"
x
13½"

1½" x 12½"

8 Join the step 7 sections to make panel D. Press the seam allowances open.

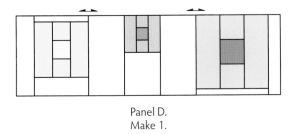

Panel D.
Make 1.

9 Sew the light-gray 1½" x 9½" rectangle to the top of the remaining medium block. Press the seam allowances open. Add the light-gray 2½" x 9½" rectangle to the bottom of the block. Press the seam allowances open. Lay out the pieced unit with the remaining large block and remaining light-gray rectangles as shown.

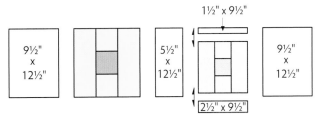

9½"
x
12½"

5½"
x
12½"

1½" x 9½"

9½"
x
12½"

2½" x 9½"

10 Sew the step 9 pieces together to make panel E. Press the seam allowances open.

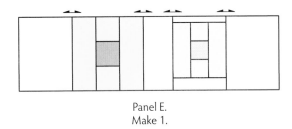

Panel E.
Make 1.

11 Refer to the quilt assembly diagram below to join panels C, D, and E. Press the seam allowances open. Add panel B to the left edge of the joined panels. Press the seam allowances open. Sew panel A to the top of the joined panels. Press the seam allowances open (fig. 1).

12 Stitch ⅛" from the edges on all four sides to prevent the edge seams from splitting open.

FINISHING

1 Cut the backing yardage into two equal lengths and sew them together to make a backing approximately 6" longer and 6" wider than the quilt top.

2 Refer to "Layering and Basting" (page 106) to layer the quilt top, batting, and backing; baste the layers together using your preferred method.

3 Using your walking foot and variegated thread, and referring to the block quilting plan below, begin by stitching in the ditch around any block. Without breaking the thread, quilt a square spiral inside the block (see page 19). End your line of quilting (see page 19) and cut your thread before moving on to the next block. Quilt all of the Square-in-a-Square blocks in the same manner to anchor the quilt (fig. 2).

Line Guides

Use painter's tape as a straight-line guide to help you quilt the square spiral. Vary the width and angle of each spiral for interest.

FIG. 1

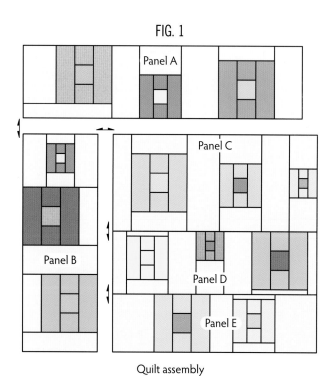

Quilt assembly

FIG. 2

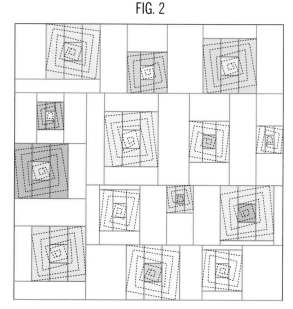

Block quilting plan

4 Remove the walking foot and attach a free-motion quilting foot. Switch to gray thread. Referring to the background quilting plan above, quilt boxes (see page 68) in the background space around the blocks. Start on one side of the quilt and work your way around all of the blocks, moving the bulk of the quilt out of the way as needed (fig. 3).

5 Refer to "Binding" (page 107) to bind the quilt edges by hand or machine using the dark-blue solid 2¼"-wide strips.

Avoid Quilting on Empty

Be sure to sew off the edge of the quilt every now and then so you can stop and check your bobbin thread level. It's much easier to put in a fresh bobbin than it is to run out of thread in the middle of the quilt!

FIG. 3

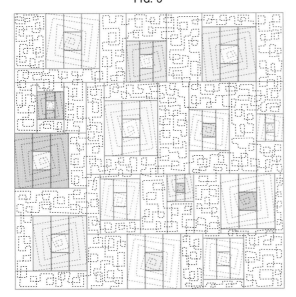

Background quilting plan

FOCAL POINT

The best tip I ever received for creating a dynamic quilt was to make sure it had a focal point. Good advice, indeed!

Quilt Details

FINISHED QUILT: 45½" x 45½"

FINISHED BLOCK: 5" x 5"

DESIGN NOTES: Eighty-one Half-Square-Triangle blocks join to create an asymmetrical quilt that looks as if it's been cropped from a larger design. The spiral quilting draws the eye across the quilt, adding just the right amount of texture to the piece.

FABRIC: Modern Neutrals by Amy Ellis, and Bella Solids, both from Moda

BATTING: Pellon Legacy Soy Blend, 50% cotton/50% soy, natural

QUILTING THREAD: Aurifil 40-weight cotton in Aluminium

MATERIALS

Yardage is based on 42"-wide fabric. Fat quarters measure approximately 18" x 21". Fat eighths measure approximately 9" x 21". For ease in piecing, label the fabrics with the letter indicated.

1 yard of cream solid (A) for background
½ yard of dark-gray geometric print (C) for blocks
½ yard of grayish-blue geometric print (E) for blocks
½ yard of medium-gray tone on tone (D) for blocks
½ yard of light-gray geometric print (I) for blocks
½ yard of gray solid (H) for blocks
⅝ yard of coral tone on tone (F) for blocks and binding
1 fat quarter of dark-gray tone on tone (G) for blocks
1 fat eighth of blue geometric print (B) for blocks
2½ yards of fabric (J) for pieced backing
50" x 50" piece of batting
Approximately 700 yards of light-gray thread for machine quilting
Washable marker
Cardboard or paper template-making material

CUTTING

From the cream solid (A), cut:
5 strips, 6" x 42"; crosscut into 25 squares, 6" x 6"

From the blue geometric print (B), cut:
1 strip, 6" x 21"; crosscut into 2 squares, 6" x 6"

From the dark-gray geometric print (C), cut:
2 strips, 6" x 42"; crosscut into 9 squares, 6" x 6"

From the medium-gray tone on tone (D), cut:
2 strips, 6" x 42"; crosscut into 8 squares, 6" x 6"

Continued on page 60

■ Designed, pieced, and quilted by Christa Watson

Continued from page 58

From the grayish-blue geometric print (E), cut:
2 strips, 6" x 42"; crosscut into 8 squares, 6" x 6"

From the coral tone on tone (F), cut:
1 strip, 6" x 42"; crosscut into 6 squares, 6" x 6"
5 strips, 2¼" x 42"

From the dark-gray tone on tone (G), cut:
2 strips, 6" x 21"; crosscut into 6 squares, 6" x 6"

From the gray solid (H), cut:
2 strips, 6" x 42"; crosscut into 10 squares, 6" x 6"

From the light-gray geometric print (I), cut:
2 strips, 6" x 42"; crosscut into 10 squares, 6" x 6"

PIECING THE BLOCKS

1 Draw a diagonal line from corner to corner on the wrong side of each A, F, and I 6" square, and one D 6" square.

2 With the marked square on top, lay an A square over each B square, right sides together. Sew ¼" from each side of the marked line. Cut the squares apart on the marked line to make four Half-Square-Triangle blocks. Press the seam allowances open.

Make 4.

3 Referring to step 2, layer the remaining A squares over each C square, seven D squares, and seven E squares. Layer the F squares over four G squares and two H squares. Layer the I squares over the remaining eight H squares and the remaining two G squares. Layer the D square over the remaining E square. Stitch, cut, and press the blocks as before to make the Half-Square-Triangle blocks shown. You will not need one A/D block, one D/E block, and one A/C block; throw them in your scrap bin to use in another project or turn them into pincushions.

Make 17.

Make 13.

Make 14.

Make 8.

Make 4.

Make 16.

Make 4.

Make 1.

4 Using a square ruler, square up each block to 5½" x 5½", keeping the 45° diagonal line of the ruler on the block seam line as you trim each side.

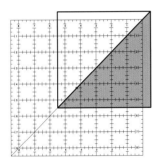

ASSEMBLING THE QUILT TOP

1 Refer to the quilt assembly diagram on page 62 to lay out the blocks in nine rows of nine blocks each.

2 Join the blocks in each row. Press the seam allowances open. Join the rows. Press the seam allowances open.

3 Stitch ⅛" from the edges on all four sides to prevent the edge seams from splitting open.

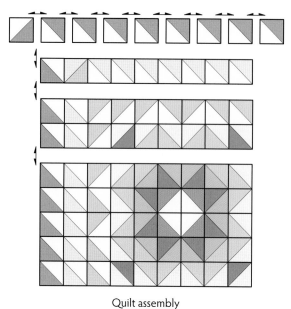

Quilt assembly

FINISHING

1 From the fabric for backing, cut one rectangle, 51½" x 40½", and two strips, 11½" x 42". Join the 11½" strips end to end and trim to 11½" x 51½". Press the seam allowances open. Join the narrow strip to the rectangle to create a backing square, 51½" x 51½".

2 Refer to "Layering and Basting" (page 106) to layer the quilt top, batting, and pieced backing; baste the layers together using your preferred method.

3 Using your walking foot and light-gray thread, quilt a continuous spiral on the quilt top (see page 20).

Centering the Spiral

To center the spiral in the middle of the star, fold the circle template made from paper (page 21) into quarters. Open it up and align the fold lines with the vertical and horizontal center seam lines of the star.

4 Refer to "Binding" (page 107) to bind the quilt edges by hand or machine using the coral 2¼"-wide strips.

Free-Motion Favorites

Free-motion quilting can add depth and texture to your quilts. In this section, I share 10 of my favorite designs that you can free-form quilt without having to mark the quilt top. Scale the designs up or down to fit your space and try combining more than one texture in the same quilt! Practice quilting these designs on a sample quilt sandwich before beginning on your actual quilt.

Before you begin quilting, take a look at the tips on page 64 to make your free-motion quilting successful. And be sure to read "Find Your Hand Position" on page 13.

■ Examples of free-motion feet: closed toe, left, and open-toe, right

Noteworthy Advice

- **CHOOSE THE RIGHT FOOT.** Select a darning foot or free-motion foot made specifically for your machine, if possible. I recommend an open-toe foot that includes a cutout for greater visibility. Some manufacturers also make generic feet that fit most machines and that can be modified.

- **DRAW BEFORE YOU QUILT.** Sketch out your quilting design on a piece of paper first to practice your muscle memory and train your brain to recognize the pattern of movement for a particular design. Draw or doodle every day for best results. Keeping a quilting journal just for drawing is a great way to develop designs and practice your "quilt handwriting."

- **QUILT DAILY.** Keep a stack of premade practice sandwiches on hand and aim to practice free-motion quilting for just 10 minutes a day. After a few days, you'll begin to see a noticeable improvement. Make up a practice sample to try out each of the quilting designs. Two 10" squares with a layer of batting in between is a great size to start with.

- **ADJUST YOUR TENSION.** If needed, adjust the tension on a practice sample using the same fabrics, batting, and thread as in your actual quilt. If the bobbin thread peeks through to the top, that means your top tension is too tight; if your top thread shows through on the back, that means your top tension is too loose.

- **USE A MATCHING THREAD COLOR.** When the thread blends into the fabric, you'll notice the texture, not the imperfections! If you're quilting over multiple fabrics, audition your threads to see which thread color blends in best. A thinner thread is less noticeable than a thicker one.

- **USE THE SAME COLOR THREAD IN THE TOP AND BOBBIN.** This helps hide any threads that are poking through on either side of the quilt, and it helps hide less-than-perfect tension.

- **TRY DIFFERENT SPEED COMBINATIONS TO FIND YOUR CORRECT RHYTHM.** This applies to your sewing-machine speed and your hand movement, which can both affect stitch quality. The secret to smooth stitching is to find the right balance. If your stitches are too small, your sewing speed is too fast for your hand speed. If your stitches are too big, you're moving your quilt faster than you're sewing. Aim for a smooth, fluid movement as you quilt.

- **GET COMFORTABLE STITCHING IN ALL DIRECTIONS.** Some people may find it easier to quilt away from themselves, while others may be more comfortable quilting toward themselves. Although free-motion quilting allows you to quilt in any direction, don't be afraid to rotate your quilt as needed for a more comfortable quilting position.

- **TRY QUILTING WITH THE FEED DOGS UP *OR* DOWN.** Although conventional wisdom says to drop your feed dogs when free-motion quilting, some machines may stitch better with them up, but covered (with a silicon mat). Try both ways to see which method you prefer.

- **REMEMBER TO MOVE AND BREATHE.** You're doing the work of the feed dogs when you move the quilt to form each stitch. To prevent this task from taking a toll on your arms and shoulders, remember to breathe (don't hold your breath!) and take breaks to get up and move around. You'll feel less fatigue and those periodic breaks will actually let you quilt for a longer cumulative time.

SIMPLE STIPPLES

One of my go-to quilting designs, stippling looks great in a variety of sizes. It can be used as an allover design or combined with other quilting motifs for added interest. Stitched large-scale, it's more commonly known as *meandering*.

To stipple, start anywhere along the edge of your practice piece, and bring the bobbin thread to the top of the quilt. Stitch a series of gently curving lines in any direction. Quilt one or two "bumps" in one direction, then slowly change directions and repeat. Continue quilting simple stipples until you've filled in the entire space.

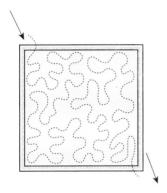

■ Detail of simple stipples on "Lightning" (page 72)

WANDERING WAVES

Similar to simple stipples, wandering waves are created by gently moving the quilt in a curving motion, but stitching in the same direction to fill a space. Make the waves as choppy or as calm as you'd like. This quilting is similar to walking-foot waves (page 18), but by free-motion quilting the waves, you can stitch in any direction you like without having to turn the quilt.

Start at the top of your practice piece. Gently move the piece from side to side while the machine stitches to create a smooth, wavy line. Quilt one line of waves at a time, stitching from top to bottom or side to side.

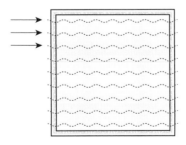

■ Detail of wandering waves on "Lightning" (page 72)

To quilt stair-step waves like I did on "Lightning" (page 72), quilt the vertical line and gently turn it into a horizontal line, curving the corner at each turn. Then move your quilt to the left or right, following the direction of the stair step. Pause again before switching directions as needed. Each line of the stair step is quilted from top to bottom.

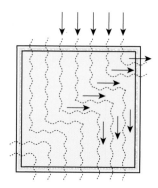

SEAWEED

Add a sharp point to the end of your wandering waves to create seaweed! Quilt lines back and forth or up and down as you fill in the space, starting and ending with sharp points.

Quilt both vertical and horizontal lines of seaweed on your practice piece. Then try combining directions—or quilting on the diagonal for even more variety.

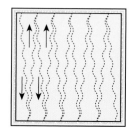 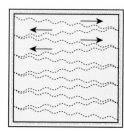

■ Detail of seaweed quilting on "Color Crystals" (page 34)

LOOPS

Loops are another quick and easy favorite that can be stitched large or small. They look great in a sashing or border, and work well as an allover design when stitched randomly in all directions across the quilt.

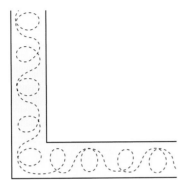

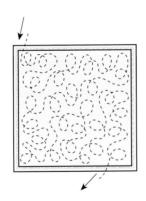

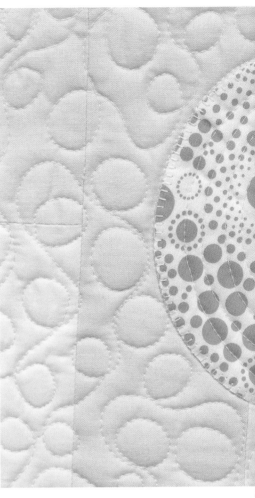

■ Detail of loops on "Candy Pop" (page 78)

To quilt loops on your practice piece, start quilting a gently curving line as if you're going to stipple. Add a circle to the line, either circling clockwise or counterclockwise. I call these *Es* and *Os*. Stitch another bit of curvy line and add your next loop. The texture looks best when switching between Es and Os each time. Practice quilting both linear loops and allover loops.

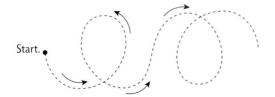

Start.

Take Aim

To quilt a continuous-loop border, start stitching in a corner at the seam. Aim to end your line of loops in the same spot, adding an extra E or O as needed.

■ Detail of boxes on "Square in a Square" (page 50)

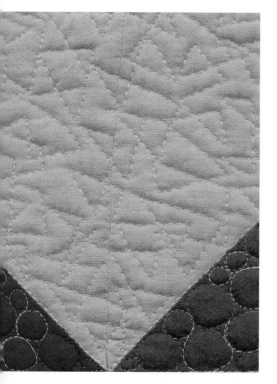

■ Detail of triangle texture on "Broken V" (page 85)

BOXES

Change your loops to squares and rectangles, and you get boxes! Don't worry about keeping your boxes perfectly square or straight. Crushed boxes are bound to happen, so embrace the irregularities of handcrafted quilting. Practice quilting boxes on a 10"-square sample. By the time you fill it up the practice square, you should have the hang of it!

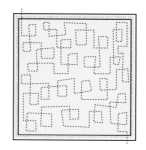
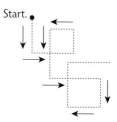

TRIANGLE TEXTURE

Triangles are another basic shape that make a great background fill. On your practice piece, begin by stitching a short straight line. Briefly pause when changing directions to form a V shape. Before closing your triangle, pivot and stitch another V shape, crossing over one of your previous lines to form a triangle. Continue to quilt sharp points and Vs, turning them into triangle shapes over the surface of your quilt. Stitch in all directions to break up the texture and to keep the pattern from looking too uniform.

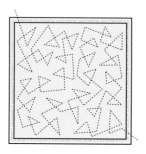
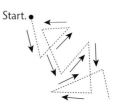

PEBBLES

Pebbles are time-consuming but they can add incredible texture to your quilts. For the "Broken V" quilt, the pebbles took nearly twice as long to quilt as the triangles did, but they covered the same amount of space—so give yourself extra time for this type of quilting. Pebbles are stitched like loops (see page 67), but without any spaces between the circles.

To quilt pebbles on your practice piece, start by bringing the thread to the top of the quilt. Immediately quilt an O shape, stitching counterclockwise. Right next to that shape, stitch another O, this time stitching clockwise. Stitch over part of the circle again if needed to get to the next position where you want to add another O. Continue adding Os right next to each other, changing directions from clockwise to counterclockwise to keep the movement fluid. Fill in all the spaces, backtracking (stitching over previous lines) if needed. Vary the size of your pebbles for interest. Don't worry if your backtracking isn't precise; the somewhat messy look adds character to the quilting!

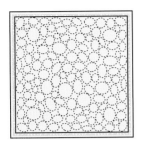 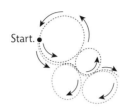

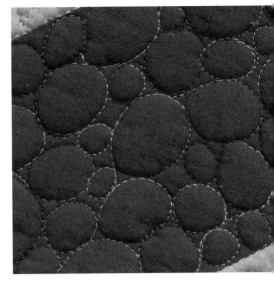

■ Detail of pebbles on "Broken V" (page 85)

SWITCHBACKS

Switchbacks are a series of back-and-forth wavy lines that can fill a lot of space quickly. Quilt them parallel for an even look, or let them bend as needed to fit in any space.

On your practice piece, draw a pair of parallel lines to represent the piecing on a quilt. These lines can represent a border, a sashing, or the background space between blocks. Starting on one edge of the space between the lines, quilt a straight line from one edge of your boundary to the other. When you have nearly touched the opposite side with your needle, begin creating a curve, and smoothly quilt back to the other side and touch it with the needle. Curve the line over to the opposite line again and repeat the motion, filling in the space. If needed, slightly change the angles of your quilted lines as your piecing angles change.

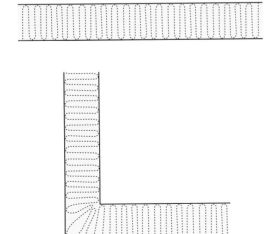

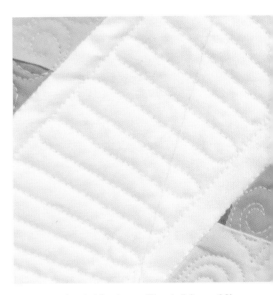

■ Detail of switchbacks on "Facets" (page 90)

Plan Ahead

If you find yourself stuck in a corner when free-motion quilting, try to quilt out of it. If there's no room to quilt, backtrack over a previous line of stitching.

FREE-MOTION SPIRALS

Spirals are fun to stitch and can be quilted large or small for completely different looks. It's easier to quilt them smoothly on a small scale, but they can add a touch of whimsy when quilted on a larger scale.

Small-Scale Spirals

To quilt small spirals, start anywhere on your practice piece and bring up your bobbin thread. Stitch two or three rounds of curves, spiraling either clockwise or counterclockwise. When you get to the center of the spiral, briefly pause, and then echo quilt your way back out of the spiral in the opposite direction.

To quilt the next spiral, continue stitching a curving line around the first spiral, and then change directions, spiraling in and out as you did before. Continue to add spirals, switching between clockwise and counterclockwise spirals at random. Add hooks and flourishes to the ends of your spirals if desired to help you switch directions and fill in the spaces.

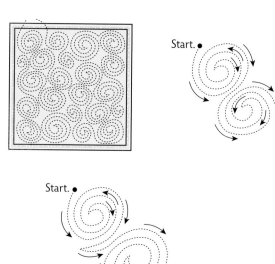

Start.

Start.

Adding flourishes

■ Detail of small-scale spirals on "Facets" (page 90)

■ Detail of large-scale spiral on "Candy Pop" (page 78)

MACHINE QUILTING WITH STYLE

Large-Scale Spirals

Spirals take on a whole new look when quilted on a larger scale inside pieced or appliquéd blocks like the dots in "Candy Pop" (page 78).

To quilt a single large spiral, start on the outer edge of your practice piece. Slowly and smoothly stitch a curve, spiraling in toward the center. Leave about ½" between the lines so that you have space between them for stitching your way back out. When you get to the center of the spiral, briefly pause and stitch back out, echoing your previous lines. This allows you to continue free-motion quilting without having to stop and break thread.

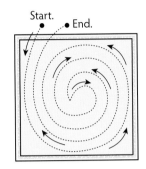

STRING OF PEARLS

This fun texture is a good way to soften the harshness of any geometric design.

Starting on the edge of your practice piece, quilt a "not-so-straight" line with your free-motion foot. Add a circle to your line, backtracking (stitching back over) part of the circle to get back to the bottom of the shape. Continue to quilt another line, and then another circle, until you reach the bottom of the piece. Move your practice piece over about ½" to 1" (or any other spacing you choose) and quilt another set of lines and circles, offsetting the circles as desired. Cut your threads at the end of each row. For a touch of irregularity, skip a circle or two. Fill in the entire space with additional strings of lines and circles.

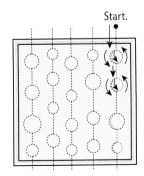

Freewheeling vs. Precision

I didn't mark the spirals on "Candy Pop." Instead, I opted for them to be free-form and somewhat imperfect. If you'd like more precise spirals, mark the lines with a water-soluble marker and stitch on the lines.

■ Detail of string-of-pearls quilting on "Pearl Gray" (page 98)

LIGHTNING

The classic Rail Fence block gets a modern makeover with improvisational piecing and a bold color scheme. Pick your favorite palette and add a pop of contrasting color to create the sleek lightning effect.

Quilt Details

FINISHED QUILT: 72½" x 96½"

FINISHED BLOCK: 12" x 12"

DESIGN NOTES: A total of 48 Modern Rail blocks are set in a 6 x 8 grid, showcasing a scrappy assortment of prints that are the perfect complement to simple quilting. The bright accents pierce the design just as a flash of lightning illuminates a darkened night.

FABRIC: Black and white prints from Robert Kaufman Fabrics, Riley Blake Designs, and my stash; Kona Cotton Solids from Robert Kaufman Fabrics in Canary and Wasabi

BATTING: Pellon Legacy Soy Blend, 50% soy/50% cotton, natural

QUILTING THREAD: Aurifil 40-weight cotton in Yellow, Aurifil 28-weight cotton in Silver Fox, and Aurifil 50-weight cotton in Dove

MATERIALS

Yardage is based on 42"-wide fabric.

Approximately ½ yard *each* of 16 assorted black, white, and gray prints for blocks*

1 yard of yellow solid for blocks

1 yard of yellow-green solid for blocks

⅔ yard of black solid for binding

6 yards of fabric for backing

76" x 100" piece of batting

Approximately 750 yards of gray thread and 300 yards of yellow thread for machine quilting

12½" x 12½" square acrylic ruler

Due to the improvisational nature of this quilt, the total amount of fabric needed may vary. Scraps can be used as long as they're at least 2½" wide and 14" long. I used more than 30 fabrics in my quilt.

CUTTING

Refer to "Cutting Wonky Wedges" (page 74) to crosscut the strips into wedges with angled sides. The total amount of wedges needed to complete the blocks will vary depending on the width they're cut. Cut fewer wedges to start, and then cut more as needed while you piece the blocks.

From the assorted black, white, and gray prints, cut a *total* of:

Approximately 16 strips, 14" x 42"; crosscut into approximately 250 to 300 wonky wedges that range from 1" x 14" to 2½" x 14"

From *each* of the yellow and the yellow-green solids, cut:

2 strips, 14" x 42"; crosscut into a *total* of 48 wonky wedges that range from 2" x 14" to 3" x 14"

From the black solid, cut:

9 strips, 2¼" x 42"

Cutting Wonky Wedges

Using a long acrylic ruler, trim the selvages from the 14" x 42" strips. Then angle the edge of the ruler to cut wedges that vary in width at the top and bottom. Use a combination of both straight and angled cuts for more variety. Some of the wedges may be narrower or wider at one end if desired. Stack up to four layers of fabric for quicker cutting.

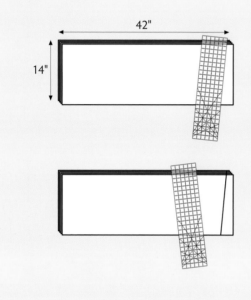

PIECING THE BLOCKS

1 Join a black, white, or gray wedge to a yellow or yellow-green wedge along the long edges. Press the seam allowances open. Repeat to make a total of 48 starter units.

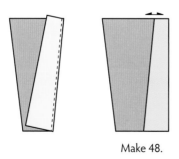

Make 48.

2 Select one starter unit. Continue adding black, white, and gray wedges to the black, white, or gray edge until the unit measures at least 13" wide. Alternate the direction you sew the seams as you add each wedge to keep the seams from bowing. Chain piece your wedges to the blocks for faster sewing. Repeat with the remaining starter units to make a total of 48 Modern Rail blocks.

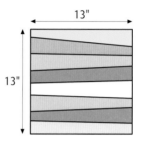

Double Up

For easier and quicker assembly, join the black, white, and gray wedges into pairs, matching the narrow end of one wedge with the wider end of another wedge.

3 Press the seam allowances of all the blocks open to reduce bulk.

4 Using the 12½" square ruler, square up each block to 12½" x 12½". If desired, turn the ruler so some of your blocks tilt slightly. To do this, lay the ruler on the block at the desired angle, making sure the 12½" line of the ruler has fabric under it on all sides. Trim along the right and top edges. Rotate the block 180° so the trimmed edges are on the left and bottom. Align the newly cut edges with the 12½"

lines of the ruler, and trim the right and top edges to square up the block.

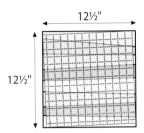

12½"

12½"

ASSEMBLING THE QUILT TOP

1 Refer to the quilt assembly diagram below to lay out the blocks in eight rows of six blocks each, alternating the direction of the wedges in each row and from row to row. Position the yellow wedges so they form lightning streaks across the quilt top.

2 Sew the blocks in each row together, joining pairs of blocks for faster sewing. Press the seam allowances open to reduce bulk, or press them in alternating directions from row to row. Join the rows to complete the quilt top. Press the seam allowances open so the top lies flat.

3 Stitch ⅛" from the edges on all four sides to prevent the edge seams from splitting open.

Quilt assembly

■ Designed, pieced, and quilted by Christa Watson

FINISHING

1 Cut the backing fabric into two equal lengths and sew them together to make a backing approximately 6" longer and 6" wider than the quilt top.

2 Refer to "Layering and Basting" (page 106) to layer the quilt top, batting, and backing; baste the layers together using your preferred method.

3 Using your walking foot, stitch in the ditch to outline the lightning streaks. Refer to the walking-foot quilting plan on page 76 and to "Color Blending" on page 76 for thread-color selection. Start stitching off of the quilt so that you don't have to secure your beginning threads. When you come to a corner, stop with the needle in the down position, lift the presser foot, and rotate the quilt, keeping as much of the bulk as possible to the left of or behind the sewing machine. Continue stitching in the ditch of the zigzag until you reach the end, and then stitch off of the quilt to end the line of stitching.

Color Blending

When stitching in the ditch, decide if you'll stitch the outlines of the lightning streaks on the yellow or black/white/gray side of the seam, and then pick the appropriate thread color. Even though this technique is called *stitch in the ditch,* it's hard to keep the stitches exactly in the ditch; by using a thread color that blends with the fabric and keeping the needle on the corresponding fabric color, any wobbles will be much less noticeable.

4 Continue working your way across the quilt, quilting the outlines of all of the zigzags to anchor the quilt. Shift the quilt as needed to keep most of the bulk away from you. When there's too much bulk in the throat space of your machine, rotate the quilt and begin stitching from the other side. Use the diagram to follow the order in which to stitch in the ditch. Rotate the quilt when beginning line #8 (fig. 1).

5 Remove the walking foot and attach a foot for free-motion quilting. Change threads to a variegated gray or one that blends with the black/white/gray areas. Quilt simple stipples (see page 65)

in the black/white/gray areas between the lightning streaks, referring to the stippling quilting plan on page 77 for a suggested quilting order. Rotate the quilt after completing section 4. If needed, check your bobbin after each section of quilting and refill it if it's low so you don't run out of thread while you're in the middle of the quilt (fig. 2).

6 Switch your thread to light yellow and refer to the wandering-waves quilting plan to quilt wandering waves (see page 65) through the zigzags with your free-motion foot. You can also do this with your walking foot if you prefer, but it will require more turning of the quilt. For variety, vary the number of lines in each wedge section (fig. 3).

7 Refer to "Binding" (page 107) to bind the quilt edges by hand or machine using the black solid 2¼"-wide strips.

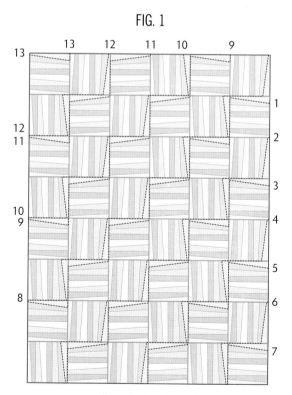

FIG. 1

Walking-foot quilting plan

FIG. 2

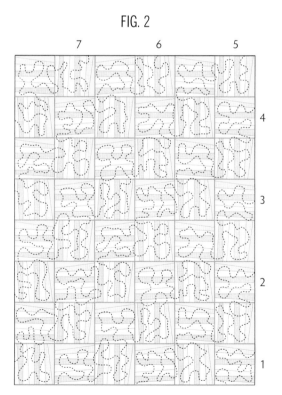

Stippling quilting plan

FIG. 3

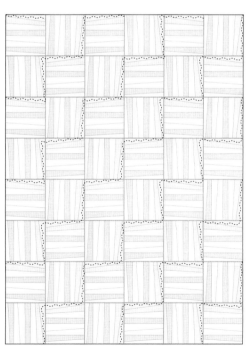

Wandering-waves quilting plan

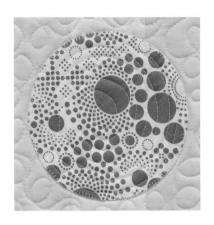

CANDY POP

This quilt reminds me of sugary-sweet treats like button dots or lollipops. It's quilted with swirls and spice and everything nice!

Quilt Details

FINISHED QUILT: 45½" x 45½"

FINISHED BLOCK: 7½" x 7½"

DESIGN NOTES: Thirty-nine brightly colored dots are machine appliquéd onto pieced blocks that are offset for interest. Scrappy leftovers create the binding, which doubles as a narrow frame. The playful quilting is accomplished as a continuous-line design.

FABRIC: Solids in Pale Pink and Pale Green and Pop prints from Riley Blake Designs

BATTING: Luna Kyoto Bamboo Blend from Moda, 50% cotton/50% bamboo, natural

APPLIQUÉ AND QUILTING THREAD: Aurifil 50-weight cotton in Light Lemon

FUSIBLE WEB: Lite Steam-A-Seam 2 from The Warm Company

MATERIALS

Yardage is based on 42"-wide fabric.

⅝ yard *each* of 6 assorted dot prints for blocks and binding

1¼ yards *each* of pale-pink and pale-green solids for blocks

3 yards of fabric for backing

50" x 50" piece of batting

Approximately 800 yards of light-yellow thread for machine appliqué and quilting

2½ yards of 18"-wide paper-backed fusible web

Template-making material such as cardstock or template plastic

Fine-tipped permanent marker

CUTTING

From *each* of the pale-pink and pale-green solids, cut:

12 strips, 3" x 42" (24 total)

From *each* of the 6 assorted dot prints, cut:

2 strips, 7" x 42" (12 total)

1 strip, 2¼" x 42" (6 total)

■ Designed, pieced, and quilted by Christa Watson

2 Using the remaining 3" x 42" strips, sew a pale-green strip to both long edges of a pale-pink strip to make strip-set B. Press the seam allowances open. Repeat to make a total of four strip sets. Crosscut the strip sets into 20 blocks, 8" wide.

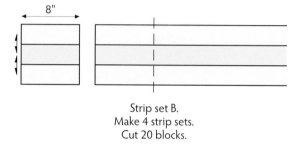

Strip set B.
Make 4 strip sets.
Cut 20 blocks.

MAKING THE BLOCKS

1 Using the 3" x 42" strips, sew a pale-pink strip to both long edges of a pale-green strip to make strip set A. Press the seam allowances open. Repeat to make a total of four strip sets. Crosscut the strip sets into 19 blocks, 8" wide.

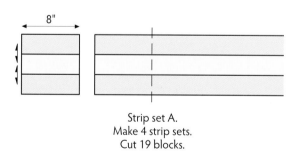

Strip set A.
Make 4 strip sets.
Cut 19 blocks.

APPLIQUÉING THE BLOCKS

1 Trace or photocopy the circle pattern (page 84) onto the template-making material. Cut out the template on the marked line.

2 Lay the circle template onto the paper side of the fusible web and trace around it with the permanent marker. Repeat to trace a total of 39 circles, leaving about ½" between each shape.

3 Roughly cut around each circle. Cut away the inside of each circle, leaving approximately ¼" of fusible web inside the drawn line.

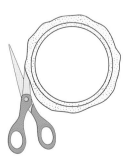

4 Following the manufacturer's instructions, adhere the rings of fusible web to the wrong side of each dot 7" x 42" strip. Fuse six fusible-web circles to three colors and seven fusible-web circles to the remaining three colors. Cut out each circle on the marked line.

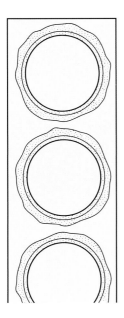

5 Remove the paper backing from one of the circle shapes. Using a ruler to help with placement, center a circle on a pieced block. The circle edges should be 1¼" to 1⅜" from the edges of the block.

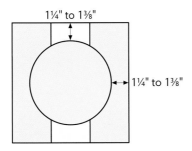

1¼" to 1⅜"

1¼" to 1⅜"

6 Once you're happy with the appliqué placement, fuse the circle permanently in place, following the manufacturer's instructions.

7 Repeat steps 5 and 6 with the remaining pieced blocks and circle appliqués.

Appliqué Tips

Follow these tips for stress-free machine appliqué.

- **STURDY SHAPES:** Templates are sturdy to trace around and create more consistent shapes than tracing directly from the book onto the fusible web. You'll also be able to trace your shapes quicker.

- **PICKING SIDES:** If you're using paper-backed, double-sided fusible web, be sure you trace on the correct paper side. Gently peel back the paper at one corner on each side of the web. Trace on the paper that sticks to the web.

- **STICKY SUBJECT:** Remember the phrase "rough to wrong." Iron the rough side (the glue side) of your fusible web to the wrong side of the fabric.

- **CAREFREE PLACEMENT:** If you don't want to fuss with exact placement, be whimsical and carefree by randomly placing your circles on the blocks. Just be sure to keep them at least ¼" away from the block edges so the appliqué doesn't get caught in the seams.

- **KEEP IT CLEAN:** Be sure to use a clean iron! If you're worried about marks or sticky residue transferring from your iron to your blocks, be sure to cover them with a Teflon pressing sheet or a large scrap of fabric.

- **WRITE IT DOWN:** Make a note of your stitch setting so you can easily switch back and forth between straight stitching and decorative stitching.

8 Select a small zigzag stitch, blanket stitch, or other decorative stitch to secure the appliqués to the blocks. Using an open-toe foot and matching or neutral thread, practice stitching on a scrap of fabric first and adjust your length and width settings until you find one you like. Take note of how each individual stitch is formed so you can anticipate where the needle will hit the fabric on each stitch. Adjust your thread tension if needed so that the bobbin thread doesn't show on the top.

9 Set the sewing machine for a straight stitch. Place the sewing-machine needle in the background fabric right next to the edge of one of the circles. Pull the bobbin thread to the top and take a series of four to five very tiny stitches to secure the threads, following the curve of the appliqué.

10 Switch to the decorative stitch and move your block slightly if needed to get the needle in the correct position. Manually turn the handwheel (always toward you, never away from you) on the machine to line up the needle so that it's ready to stitch in the background fabric right next to the appliqué.

11 Stitch around the circle, keeping the thread on the surface of the appliqué fabric and along the edge of the appliqué, following the curve of the shape. If your machine comes with a knee lift, use it to keep your hands free so that they can gently turn your block as you stitch.

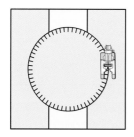

12 When you've stitched completely around the circle, switch back to a straight stitch and secure the threads with a series of tiny stitches along the edge of the shape. Clip the threads.

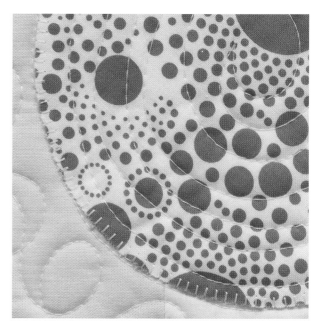

■ Candy Pop block that's been machine appliquéd with a blanket stitch.

Knot Secure

If you prefer a cleaner look, start and end with long thread tails. Pull the tails through to the back, and then tie the ends in a knot to secure them.

13 Repeat steps 9–12 to appliqué the remaining blocks.

Stable Stitches

If desired, use a sheet or two of tear-away stabilizer on the back of each block as you stitch to keep the stitches flat and pucker free. I didn't find it necessary to use stabilizer with these big shapes; the fusible was enough to stabilize my blocks as I stitched.

14 Very carefully, trim away the block fabric behind the appliqué on each block, leaving a ¼" seam allowance. Be careful not to cut through the appliqués. This will prevent shadowing of your background fabric in addition to reducing bulk.

ASSEMBLING THE QUILT TOP

1 Refer to the row assembly diagram below to lay out the blocks in six vertical rows as shown, alternating rows of six block with rows of seven blocks and staggering the blocks. The background stripe colors should alternate and the blocks should all be oriented with the stripes running vertically (fig. 1).

2 Trim the six blocks on the ends of the seven-block rows to measure 4¼" x 8". Be sure to trim across the width of the block, perpendicular to the background strips, so that the stripes remain vertical. Place the trimmed blocks back in position.

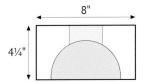

Cut Carefully!

Don't just cut the end blocks in half; if you do, the seam allowances will be missing and the blocks will be too small. The extra ¼" ensures a full half circle will show at each end of the alternate rows.

3 Refer to the quilt assembly diagram below. Sew the blocks in each vertical row together. Press the seam allowances open. Join the rows. Press the seam allowances open (fig. 2).

4 Stitch ⅛" from the edges on all four sides to prevent the edge seams from splitting open.

FINISHING

1 Cut the backing yardage into two equal lengths and sew them together to make a backing approximately 6" longer and 6" wider than the quilt top. For a creative touch, make a few extra blocks from your leftovers and piece them into the backing.

FIG. 1

Row assembly

FIG. 2

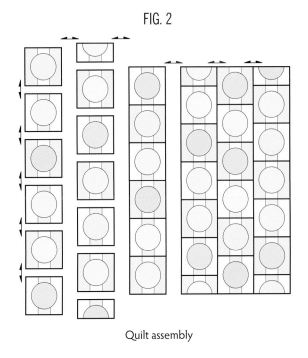

Quilt assembly

2 Refer to "Layering and Basting" (page 106) to layer the quilt top, batting, and backing; baste the layers together.

3 Using a free-motion foot and the light-yellow thread, start in any corner of the quilt and free-motion quilt a series of meandering loops (page 67). When you reach an appliquéd circle, stitch around the outside of the circle. Without breaking the thread, continue quilting in toward the center of the circle, creating a spiral (page 70). When you reach the center of the circle, briefly pause and quilt back out of the circle, echoing your previous lines. Continue stitching loops and spirals across the quilt top to complete the quilting. See page 70 for a detailed close-up.

4 Join the dot 2¼"-wide strips end to end to make one long strip. Refer to "Binding" (page 107) to bind the quilt edges by hand or machine using the pieced strip.

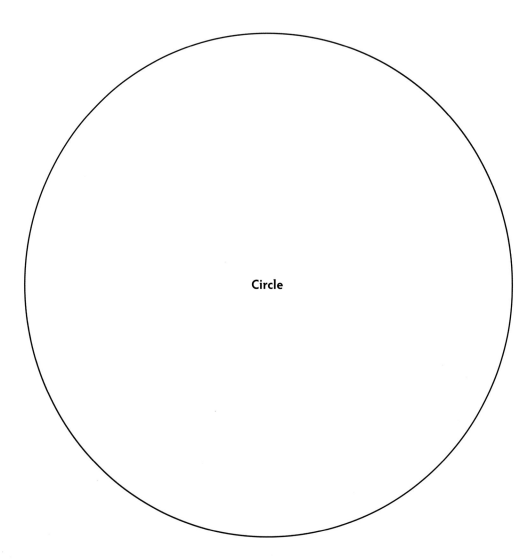

Circle

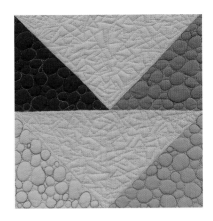

BROKEN V

Half-square triangles are the building blocks of many fabulous quilts, and they're fun to quilt too! Play around with the basic unit and see what other designs you can create!

Quilt Details

FINISHED QUILT: 60½" x 70½"

FINISHED BLOCK: 10" x 10"

DESIGN NOTES: A total of 168 half-square-triangle units are sewn together in matching pairs to create Double Diamond blocks that form an asymmetrical design. Incredible texture is added to the quilt through the use of two contrasting free-motion quilting patterns. Consider adding additional quilting motifs for more variety.

FABRIC: Shot Cottons by Kaffe Fassett for Rowan by Westminster Fibers

BATTING: Quilters Dream Wool, 100% wool, natural

QUILTING THREAD: Aurifil 50-weight cotton in Aluminium and Marrakesh

SPECIALTY RULER: 6½" Triangle Square Up Ruler (optional)

MATERIALS

Yardage is based on 42"-wide fabric. Fat quarters measure approximately 18" x 21".

1 fat quarter *each* of 14 assorted solids for blocks
3 yards of gray solid for blocks
⅝ yard of light-purple solid for binding
4 yards of fabric for backing
66" x 76" piece of batting
Approximately 1000 yards *each* of gray and variegated thread for machine quilting
6½" Triangle Square Up Ruler (optional)

CUTTING

From *each* of the 14 assorted solid fat quarters, cut:
2 strips, 6" x 21"; crosscut into 6 squares, 6" x 6" (84 total)

From the gray solid, cut:
14 strips, 6" x 42"; crosscut into 84 squares, 6" x 6"

From the light-purple solid, cut:
7 strips, 2¼" x 42"

PIECING THE BLOCKS

1 Mark a diagonal line from corner to corner on the wrong side of each gray square.

2 With right sides together, lay a marked gray square over a colored square. Sew ¼" from both sides of the marked line. Cut the squares apart on the drawn line to make two half-square-triangle units. Repeat with the remaining gray and solid squares to make a

MACHINE QUILTING WITH STYLE

total of 168 half-square-triangle units. Do not press the seam allowances yet. Keep pairs of matching units together.

■ Designed, pieced, and quilted by Christa Watson

3 If you're using the Triangle Square Up Ruler, follow the instructions in "Trimming Trick" at right to square up each half-square-triangle unit before it's pressed. Otherwise, press the seam allowances of each unit open, and then trim each unit to 5½" x 5½", keeping the seam line centered diagonally.

4 Join two matching half-square-triangle units as shown to make an A unit. Repeat to make a total of 28 A units. Press the seam allowances open.

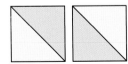 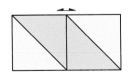

Unit A.
Make 28.

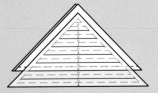

5 Join two matching half-square-triangle units as shown to make a B unit. Repeat to make a total of 56 B units. Press the seam allowances open.

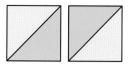 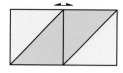

Unit B.
Make 56.

6 Join two A units as shown to make block A. Repeat to make a total of 14 A blocks. Press the seam allowances open.

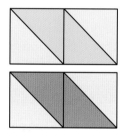 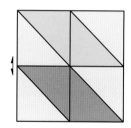

Block A.
Make 14.

7 Join two B units as shown to make block B. Repeat to make a total of 28 B blocks. Press the seam allowances open.

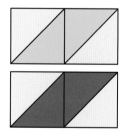 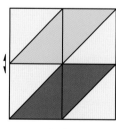

Block B.
Make 28.

ASSEMBLING THE QUILT TOP

1 Refer to the quilt assembly diagram to lay out the blocks in six vertical rows of seven blocks each as shown, using the A blocks in the first two rows and the B blocks in the remaining rows.

2 Sew the blocks in each row together. Press the seam allowances open. Join the rows to complete the quilt top. Press the seam allowances open.

3 Stitch ⅛" away from the edges on all four sides to prevent the edge seams from splitting open.

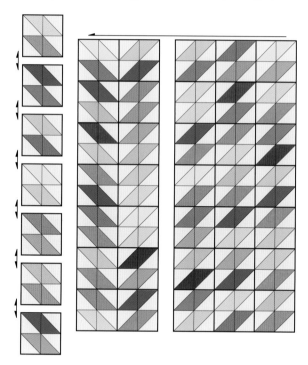

Quilt assembly

FINISHING

1 Cut the backing yardage into two equal lengths and sew them together to make a backing approximately 6" longer and 6" wider than the quilt top.

2 Refer to "Layering and Basting" (page 106) to layer the quilt top, batting, and backing; baste the layers together using your preferred method. If you use wool batting like I did, I recommend pin basting rather than spray basting.

3 Using gray thread and a walking foot and referring to the walking-foot quilting plan on page 89, stitch in the ditch following the black numbered lines in the diagram. Start and stop your lines of quilting off of the quilt so that you don't have to secure your threads. Keep the bulk of the quilt to the left of the needle and pivot the quilt where lines meet to stitch in the opposite direction. Rotate the quilt as needed to complete the lines of quilting.

4 Next, stitch in the ditch following the red lettered lines, rotating the quilt as needed when it gets too bulky. Your quilt is now anchored and ready for free-motion quilting on any section (fig. 1).

5 Remove the walking foot and attach a free-motion quilting foot. Referring to the free-motion quilting plan below, quilt triangle texture (see page 68) into the background areas using matching gray thread. Work in columns from top to bottom without cutting the threads from one block to the next. Start and end your quilting session off the quilt to avoid needing to bury your threads.

Bobbin Along

Stop and check your bobbin thread after every one or two columns. When it's getting low, replace it with a full bobbin so you don't run out of thread in the middle of a stitching session. If you do run out of thread at an inopportune time, see "Starting and Ending a Line of Quilting" (page 19) for blending your stitches so there's no obvious starting or stopping point.

6 Using variegated thread, quilt a pebble motif in each of the colored diamonds, again without cutting the threads until you've quilted an entire column. Quilt each column from top to bottom, rotating the quilt halfway through to finish (fig. 2).

7 Refer to "Binding" (page 107) to bind the quilt edges by hand or machine using the light-purple 2¼"-wide strips.

FIG. 1

21 20 19 18 17 16 15

14 13 12 11 10 9 8 7 6 5 4 3 2 1

A B C D E F G H I J K L M

24 23 22

Start

Walking-foot quilting plan

FIG. 2

Free-motion quilting plan

FACETS

Break free from the monotony of repetitive blocks by using your smallest scraps to make your own fabric. Accent the design by using both walking-foot and free-motion quilting techniques.

MATERIALS

Yardage is based on 42"-wide fabric. Fat eighths measure approximately 9" x 21".

28 fat eighths OR approximately 3½" yards of scraps of assorted red, orange, yellow, and green solids for blocks*
2⅞ yards of white solid for blocks**
1⅛ yards of red solid for accent blocks and binding**
4½ yards of fabric for backing
70" x 77" piece of batting
Approximately 1000 yards of white, 1200 yards of yellow, and 150 yards of red thread for machine quilting
Template-making material OR Creative Grids Triangle Squared Ruler and Perfect Rectangle Ruler

* Due to the improvisational nature of this quilt, the total amount of fabric you need may vary. The more fabrics you use, the better.

** These amounts are for use with the rulers. If you're using the half-rectangle and triangle patterns (pages 96 and 97) instead, purchase ½ yard more than the amount given.

Using the Perfect Rectangle Ruler

1. Once strips are cut, keep them folded so they're two layers thick; this will ensure you cut a pair of half-rectangles—one right facing and one left facing—with each cut.

2. Align the 7½" line of the ruler with the bottom edge of the fabric strip. The top of the ruler should align with the top edge of the strip.

3. Rotary cut along the straight edge of the ruler to cut the first angle.

4. Rotary cut along the diagonal edge of the ruler to form the half-rectangle shape.

5. With the ruler still in place, trim off the upper-left tip of the triangle to create the blunted tip.

6. Rotate the ruler 180° so the diagonal edge lines up with the last cut and the blunted tip is aligned with the bottom edge of the strip.

7. Cut along the straight edge to release the triangles, and then trim the tip to blunt it as you did in step 5.

8. Continue rotating the ruler and cutting the pairs, using additional strips as needed, until you have the required number of triangles.

9. Separate the triangles into left-facing and right-facing triangles.

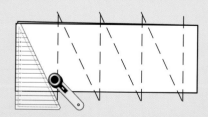

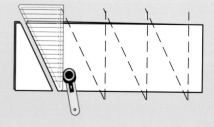

Using the Triangle Squared Ruler

1. Keep the solid fabric strips folded so you can cut two triangles at once. Cut through a single layer of crazy-pieced strips.

2. Align the 7½" line of the ruler with the bottom edge of the fabric strip. The blunted point of the ruler should be aligned with the top edge of the strip.

3. Rotary cut along the left edge of the ruler to cut the first triangle edge.

4. Rotary cut along the right edge of the ruler to release the triangles.

5. Rotate the ruler 180° so the 7½" line is aligned with the top edge of the fabric strip and the diagonal edge is aligned with the last cut.

6. Cut along the right edge of the ruler to release the next pair of triangles.

7. Continue rotating the ruler and releasing pairs of triangles, using additional strips as needed, until you have the required number of triangles.

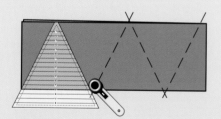

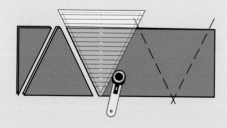

CUTTING

If you're using the specialty rulers to cut the half-rectangles and triangles, refer to "Using the Triangle Squared Ruler" and "Using the Perfect Rectangle Ruler" (page 92) before cutting the pieces. If you're making templates, trace the patterns (pages 96 and 97) onto template-making material and cut them out. Use the templates to cut the pieces.

From the assorted red, orange, yellow, and green fat eighths or scraps, cut:

Various-sized strips, squares, rectangles, and chunks of fabric. The pieces don't need to be cut in even sizes or regular shapes; however, all sides should be cut straight with a ruler.

From the white solid, cut:

12 strips, 7½" x 42". Use the Perfect Rectangle Ruler or the half-rectangle template to cut the strips into 90 left-facing half-rectangles and 90 right-facing half-rectangles.

From the red solid, cut:

2 strips, 7½" x 42". Use the Triangle Squared Ruler or the triangle template to cut the strips into 10 triangles.

8 strips, 2¼" x 42"

MAKING THE CRAZY-PIECED TRIANGLES

1 Randomly sew the assorted red, orange, yellow, and green pieces together to create larger Crazy-pieced chunks of fabric. Press the seam allowances open where possible, or press in the direction that's easiest.

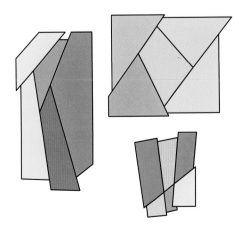

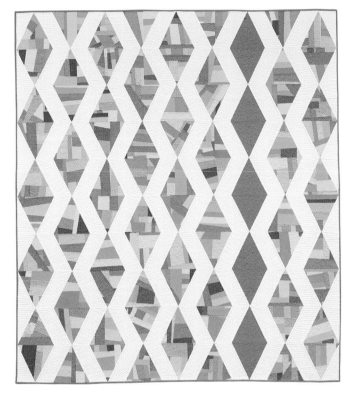

■ Designed, pieced, and quilted by Christa Watson

2 Cut apart some the pieces in step 1 and resew them to other pieces as desired to make a pieced unit at least 17" x 21". Press the seam allowances open where possible. Make a total of 10 crazy-pieced units. Starch the finished pieces if desired to make them easier to work with. Trim the units for cutting.

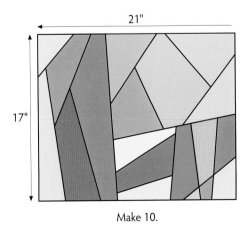

21"

17"

Make 10.

3 From each of the Crazy-pieced units, cut two strips, 7½" x 21" (20 total). Use the Triangle Squared Ruler or the triangle template to cut a total of 80 triangles from the strips. You should be able to cut four triangles from each Crazy-pieced strip.

Cut 80.

MAKING THE BLOCKS

1 Sew white half-rectangles to both sides of a Crazy-pieced triangle, matching up the blunted ends at the bottom of the triangles. The tip of the Crazy-pieced triangle should extend above the top of the white triangle on one side only. Press the seam allowances open. Repeat to make a total of 80 Crazy-pieced blocks.

Make 80.

2 Repeat step 1 with the red-solid triangles and remaining white half-rectangles to make a total of 10 red blocks.

Make 10.

ASSEMBLING THE QUILT TOP

1 Refer to the quilt assembly diagram below to lay out nine vertical rows of 10 blocks each as shown, alternating the direction of the block tips in each row and from row to row.

2 Sew the blocks in each vertical row together. Press the seam allowances open. Join the rows. Press the seam allowances open.

3 Stitch ⅛" from the edges on all four sides to prevent the edge seams from splitting open.

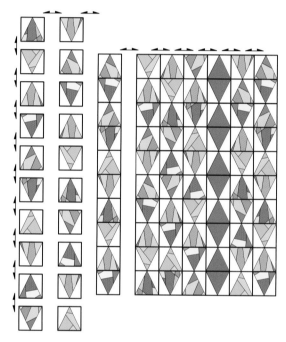

Quilt assembly

FINISHING

1 Cut the backing fabric into two equal lengths and sew them together to make a backing approximately 6" longer and wider than the quilt top.

2 Refer to "Layering and Basting" (page 106) to layer the quilt top, batting, and backing; baste the layers together.

3 Using your walking foot and white thread, refer to figure 1 on page 95 to stitch in the ditch along the diagonal lines of each triangle to anchor the quilt. When you reach the center, rotate the quilt 180°

and continue stitching in the ditch to outline all the diamonds. After all of the anchor quilting has been done, you can quilt the rest of the quilt in any order.

Work Order

When stitching in the ditch, always quilt your lines from top to bottom to reduce the chance of puckering. Don't rotate the quilt for each row of quilting.

4 Using the edge of your walking foot as a guide, quilt linear echoes (page 16) approximately ¼" to ⅜" from the ditch quilting lines, starting and ending off the quilt as before. There's no need to mark these lines, just stitch slowly and evenly. This will create a channel of unquilted space that really pops (fig. 1).

5 Attach a free-motion quilting foot. Refer to figure 2 below to fill in the white spaces with switchbacks (page 69) using matching thread. Don't be concerned about making the switchbacks perfectly spaced or evenly stitched. Quilt each row of switchbacks in one sitting for consistency, starting and stopping off the edge of the quilt. Cut the threads in between each row of quilting before going on to the next. When quilting the outer white triangles, stop quilting ¼" away from the edges.

6 Switch to the yellow thread and quilt small-scale spirals (page 70) through each row of Crazy-pieced diamonds. Start at the top of a column and work toward the bottom of the quilt without cutting the thread between blocks. Use red thread to quilt the column of red diamonds in the same manner (fig. 2).

7 Refer to "Binding" (page 107) to bind the quilt edges with the red 2¼"-wide strips.

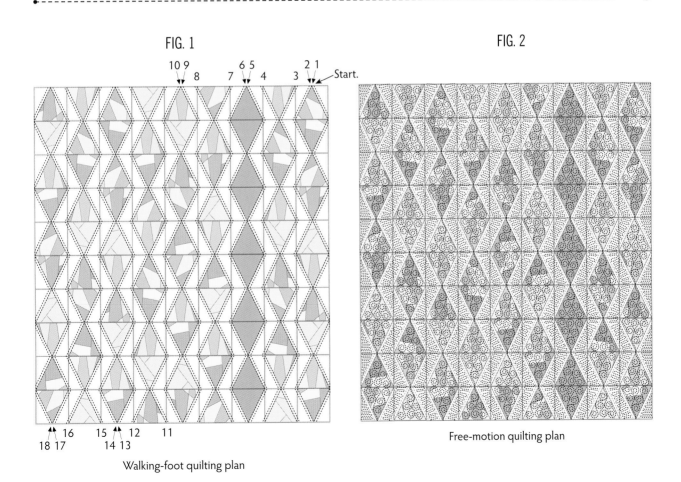

FIG. 1

Walking-foot quilting plan

FIG. 2

Free-motion quilting plan

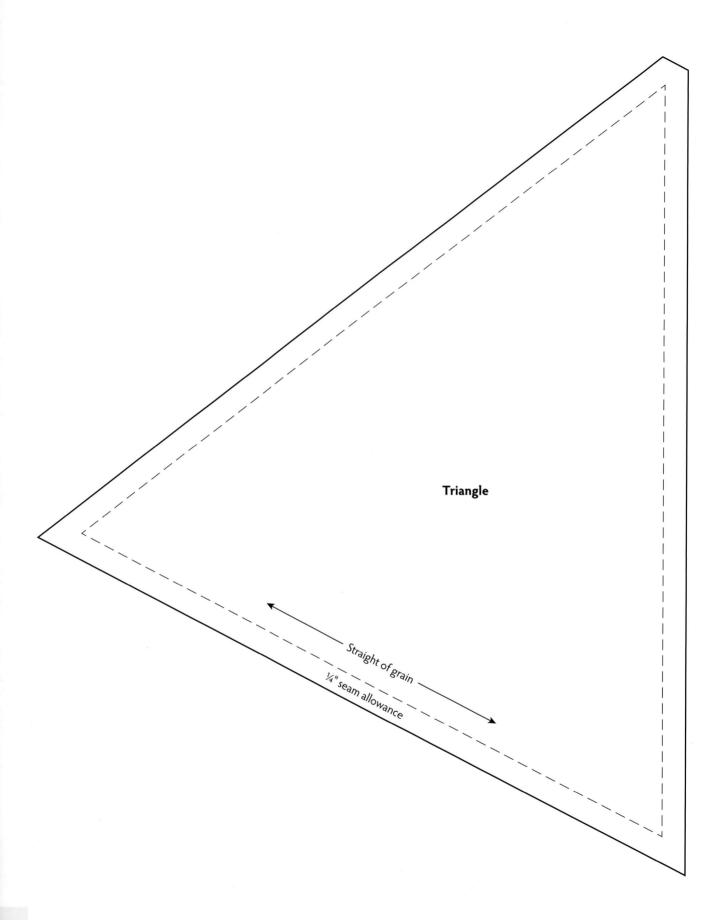

Triangle

Straight of grain

¼" seam allowance

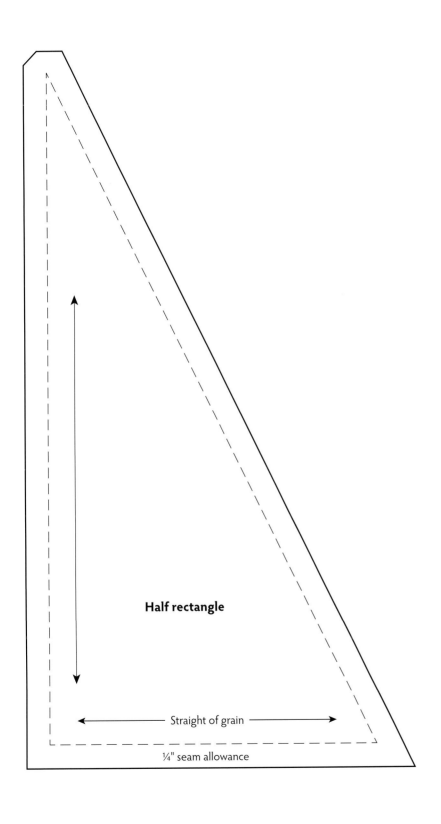

Half rectangle

Straight of grain

¼" seam allowance

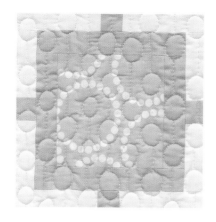

PEARL GRAY

Showcase your favorite set of fabrics all in the same quilt! Frame them in subtle grays and white for a dynamic grid look.

Quilt Details

FINISHED QUILT: 66½" x 77½"

FINISHED BLOCK: 11" x 11"

DESIGN NOTES: A total of 42 Pearl blocks are set side by side in a 6 x 7 grid. By using two different background solids, a secondary checkerboard design emerges. Leftover scraps are used in the binding, and the "string of pearls" quilting motif adds another layer of design to the piece.

FABRIC: Pearl Bracelets by Lizzy House for Andover Fabrics, Kona Cotton Solids by Robert Kaufman Fabrics

BATTING: The Warm Company Warm & Natural for the bottom layer, 100% cotton, natural; Pellon Legacy for the top layer, 100% wool, natural

QUILTING THREAD: Superior Threads Fantastico 40-weight trilobal polyester in White

MATERIALS

Yardage is based on 42"-wide fabric. Fat eighths measure approximately 9" x 21".

2⅛ yards of medium-gray solid for block accents
15 fat eighths of assorted prints for block centers and binding
1¾ yards of dark-gray solid for block backgrounds
1¾ yards of white solid for block backgrounds
5 yards of fabric for backing
71" x 82" piece of batting (or two pieces if using a double batting)
Approximately 1000 yards of white thread for machine quilting

CUTTING

From *each* of 14 of the assorted fat eighths, cut:
1 strip, 2¼" x 21" (14 total)

From the remainder of the fat eighths, cut a *total* of:
42 squares, 5½" x 5½"

From the medium-gray solid, cut:
12 strips, 1½" x 42"
4 strips, 5½" x 42"; crosscut into 84 rectangles, 1½" x 5½"
4 strips, 7½" x 42"; crosscut into 84 rectangles, 1½" x 7½"

From the dark-gray solid, cut:
6 strips, 3½" x 42"
6 strips, 5½" x 42"

From the white solid, cut:
6 strips, 3½" x 42"
6 strips, 5½" x 42"

■ Designed, pieced, and quilted by Christa Watson

Chain Sew for Efficiency

For efficiency, chain piece all of the gray rectangles on one side of the squares first, and then chain piece the rectangles on the opposite sides of the squares before pressing.

PIECING THE BLOCKS

1 Sew medium-gray 1½" x 5½" rectangles to the sides of each assorted print 5½" square. Press the seam allowances open. Add medium-gray 1½" x 7½" rectangles to the top and bottom of each square. Press the seam allowances open.

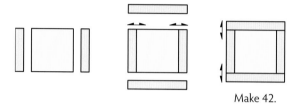

Make 42.

2 Sew dark-gray 3½" x 42" strips to both long edges of a medium-gray 1½" x 42" strip to make strip set A. Repeat to make a total of three strip sets. Press the seam allowances open. Crosscut the strip sets into 42 segments, 2½" wide.

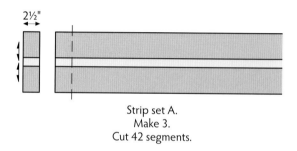

Strip set A.
Make 3.
Cut 42 segments.

3 Sew dark-gray 5½" x 42" strips to both long edges of a medium-gray 1½" x 42" strip to make strip set B. Repeat to make a total of three strip sets. Press the seam allowances open. Crosscut the strip sets into 42 segments, 2½" wide.

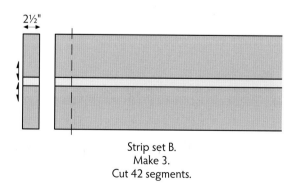

Strip set B.
Make 3.
Cut 42 segments.

4 Sew white 3½" x 42" strips to both long edges of a medium-gray 1½" x 42" strip to make strip set C. Repeat to make a total of three strip sets. Press the seam allowances open. Crosscut the strip sets into 42 segments, 2½" wide.

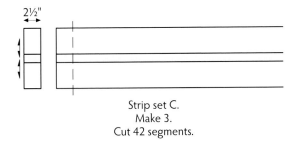

2½"

Strip set C.
Make 3.
Cut 42 segments.

5 Sew white 5½" x 42" strips to both long edges of a medium-gray 1½" x 42" strip to make strip set D. Repeat to make a total of three strip sets. Press the seam allowances open. Crosscut the strip sets into 42 segments, 2½" wide.

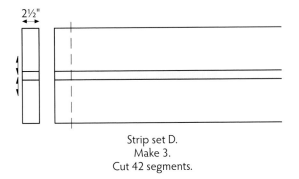

2½"

Strip set D.
Make 3.
Cut 42 segments.

6 Sew A segments to opposite sides of 21 units from step 1. Press the seam allowances open. Sew B segments to the top and bottom of these units to make 21 dark-gray blocks. Press the seam allowances open.

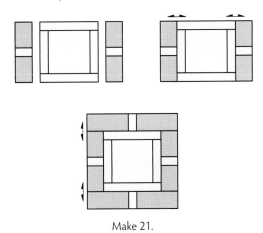

Make 21.

7 Repeat step 6 with the remaining units from step 1 and the C and D segments to make 21 white blocks.

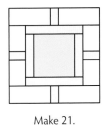

Make 21.

ASSEMBLING THE QUILT TOP

1 Refer to the quilt assembly diagram on page 102 to lay out the blocks in seven rows of six blocks each, alternating the white and gray blocks in each row and from row to row.

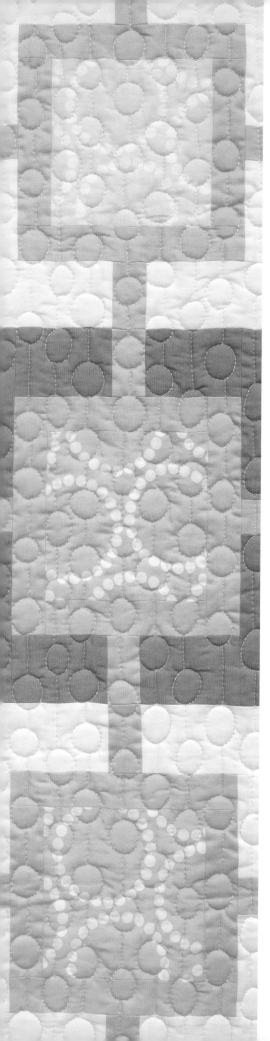

2 Sew the blocks in each row together. Press the seam allowances open. Sew the rows together. Press the seam allowances open.

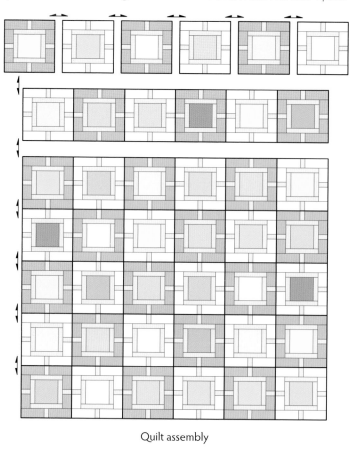

Quilt assembly

3 Stitch ⅛" from the edges on all four sides to prevent the edge seams from splitting open.

FINISHING

1 Cut the backing yardage into two equal lengths and sew them together to make a backing that's approximately 6" longer and 6" wider than the quilt top.

2 Refer to "Layering and Basting" (page 106) to layer the quilt top, batting, and backing; baste the layers together using your preferred method.

3 Using a free-motion foot and a thread that blends with the fabrics, refer to "String of Pearls" (page 71) and the free-motion quilting plan on page 103 to quilt the quilt top. Starting on the right-hand side of the quilt, quilt a string of pearls design through the vertical center of the far-right block row, shown in red on the diagram. Quilt through the vertical center of each block row to anchor the quilt, working across the quilt

until you reach the midpoint. Rotate the quilt 180°, begin quilting at the midway point where you left off, and continue working from top to bottom through the block centers across the quilt.

Choosing Thread Color

Quilt with one type of thread in a color that blends with the fabrics so that your eye sees the overall *texture* of the quilting, not the individual stitches.

4 Starting at the upper-right corner of the quilt, fill in between the previous rows of quilted strings with additional rows, shown in black on the diagram. Vary the spacing between each string for variety. I quilted 11 vertical rows of strings per column of blocks, each about 1" wide. When you reach the midpoint of the quilt, rotate the quilt again and start quilting where you left off, working toward the outer edge.

5 Join the assorted-print 2¼" x 21" strips end to end to make one long strip. Refer to "Binding" (page 107) to bind the quilt edges by hand or machine using the pieced strip.

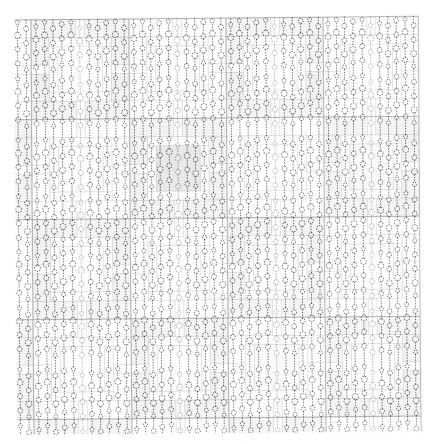

Free-motion quilting plan

Finishing Touches

The main focus of this book is the actual quilting process, but before and after the quilting is done, there are other steps that need to be taken. This section gives instructions for making a pieced backing, layering and basting the quilt sandwich, binding the edges, and attaching a label.

PIECED BACKINGS

Pieced backings are a fun way to personalize your quilt and to take an interesting element from the quilt front and incorporate it into another design on the back. If you plan to have your quilt professionally quilted rather than doing it yourself, you may want to make your backings a few inches larger than the sizes listed in this book. The following design is a great way to use up those leftover hunks 'n' chunks—just sew them together into larger units until you've got a big enough backing. For a different-sized quilt, adjust the number of rows as needed, and substitute the blue, aqua, and gray scraps with fabrics that coordinate with your quilt front.

Materials

Approximately 3½ yards *total* of blue and aqua scraps
Approximately 2¾ yards *total* of gray scraps

Making the Backing

1 Cut the scraps into 11"-wide pieces as long as the scrap will allow. If your scraps are less than 11" wide, cut them as wide as possible and then join as many same-color pieces as necessary to make an 11"-wide piece.

2 Join the blue and aqua 11"-wide pieces end to end to make a strip 96" long. Make four pieced strips. Repeat with the gray pieces to make three pieced strips.

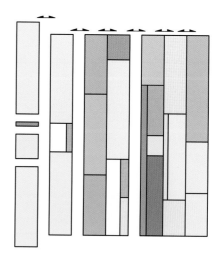

3 Join the strips along the long edges, alternating colors. Reverse the sewing direction as you add each strip to prevent the strips from bowing. Press the seam allowances open.

■ Back of "Ripples" (page 22). Finished Size: 74" x 96"

LAYERING AND BASTING

Once your quilt top is pieced, the batting has been selected, and the backing has been made, it's time to layer the pieces and baste them together. This process is easier and less time consuming if you have someone to help you... but then, most jobs are!

I baste all of my quilts on two large plastic tables that have been pushed together. The tables are 30" x 96" and fold up for easy storage. I've also successfully used my kitchen table or even a smaller cutting table for basting; just shift the quilt as needed.

Two basting methods I like to use are basting with safety pins and basting with temporary spray adhesive. For either basting method, you'll need to give your quilt top and backing a final press before beginning the layering process. The batting should also be wrinkle free. For packaged batting, remove it from the packaging several days before you plan to use it and spread it on a flat surface, like a bed, to allow it to relax. You can also throw the batting in a dryer on a fluff or no-heat setting for about 10 minutes to remove the wrinkles. Some cotton and cotton-blend battings can be ironed on a low-heat setting, but you should always consult the manufacturer's information and test on a corner of the batting to make sure no melting occurs. Cotton battings sometimes have a polyester scrim layer applied to them to keep the cotton fibers from separating; ironing this layer can alter your batting.

Safety-Pin Basting

1 Lay the quilting backing wrong side up on your work surface and tape the edges to the table with several pieces of painter's tape. If the backing is too long or wide, let the excess hang off the table evenly on both sides and just tape the sides where the table is exposed. You want the backing to lie smooth and even on the table, but you don't want to stretch it taut.

2 Lay the batting on top of the backing, ensuring that you can see the backing on all four edges underneath. Smooth the batting into place if needed.

3 Lay the quilt top right side up over the batting. Try to center the quilt so you have an even amount of backing sticking out on all sides of the quilt. Smooth out all three layers.

4 Starting on one edge of the quilt, safety pin all three layers together every 2" to 3". Pin as large of a section as you can comfortably reach, then go back and close all of your pins. Move to another section of your quilt sandwich, pin, and close the pins. Pin the entire section on the table, and then if any part of the quilt is hanging off the table, remove the tape, shift the quilt, retape the backing to the table, and continue pinning until the entire quilt sandwich is pinned together.

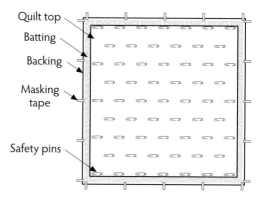

Quilt top
Batting
Backing
Masking tape
Safety pins

Pin Pointer

Sprinkle a bunch of safety pins over the surface of the quilt top so they're easy to pick up and pin. I use a Kwik Klip tool to fasten the safety pins quickly while also sparing my fingers and nails.

Spray Basting

I prefer to spray baste my quilts because it ensures that every part of the quilt is sticking together and there are no pesky pins to remove while quilting. However, the downside is that basting spray is more expensive than pins, it needs to be done outside or in a well-ventilated room, and it doesn't work well with all battings.

Battings that repel water, such as wool, may not interact well with the spray. Test a piece of batting first before you attempt to use the spray on an entire quilt. In my experience, 505 Spray and Fix works the best with 100% cotton and cotton-blend battings. My spray-basting technique is slightly different from what it says to do on the product instructions, so be sure to test it on a smaller piece to ensure this method will work for you. Or, spray outside, but bring your quilt pieces inside to assemble.

1 Lay a protective cloth, such as a bed sheet, over the surface of your table, or the ground, to protect it from overspray. You may also want to put down a ground cloth to protect your flooring if you're basting indoors.

2 Lay the quilt backing wrong side up on your work surface, and apply an even coating of spray over the surface of the backing. If the backing is larger than the work surface, spray it in sections.

3 Gently move the backing from the work area and drape it over a low wall, a couch, or other surface where it won't be touched for a few minutes. Drape it sprayed side up.

4 Lay the quilt top wrong side up on the work surface and apply an even coating of spray, just like you did for the backing.

5 Gently move the top out of the way and remove the protective covering from the work surface.

6 Lay the backing on the work area, wrong side up, and tape down the edges with painter's tape. If the backing is too long or wide, let the excess hang off the table evenly on both sides and just tape the sides where the table is exposed. You want the backing to lie smooth and even on the table, but you don't want to stretch it taut.

7 Place the batting on the quilt backing. You can lift up the batting if needed to reposition it. Smooth out the batting, if needed, and work out the bumps.

8 Place the quilt top on the batting. It may help to fold the top right sides together and center it over the center of your backing, and then smooth it in place one side at a time with a helper.

9 Use a long acrylic ruler to help you smooth out the top so it's flat and square. As you smooth, use the ruler as a straight edge to tug the quilt into alignment if needed. The layers should be gently secure.

10 Take the quilt sandwich to your ironing board and press the back with a hot, dry iron to smooth out any wrinkles and set the glue. Be sure to test first to ensure your batting doesn't melt or scorch.

11 Flip the quilt over and iron the front in the same manner. Your quilt is now ready to machine quilt.

BINDING

All of my quilts are bound the same way using continuous length, double-fold, straight-grain binding. That's a mouthful, but it works great! I cut my strips 2¼" wide, perpendicular to the selvage, and use ¼" seam allowances throughout. This produces a binding that finishes approximately ⅜" wide.

1 Use a large square ruler to trim the quilt corners to 90° if needed. Use a long ruler to trim the sides even, and to trim the batting and backing flush with the quilt-top edges.

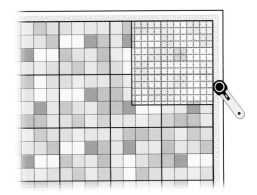

2 Calculate the number of binding strips needed by measuring the perimeter of the quilt and adding 10" for joining strips and mitering corners. For example, for a quilt that measures 60" x 80", the measurement would be calculated as:
60 + 60 + 80 + 80 + 10 = 290.

Divide this measurement by 40" and round up to the nearest whole number. In this case, the number of strips to cut would be eight.

3 Join the strips into one continuous length. With right sides together, overlap two strips at a 90° angle, with each strip end slightly extending beyond the other strip. Stitch diagonally across the strips, beginning and ending where the strips intersect and create a V. Trim the excess, leaving a ¼" seam allowance. Press the seam allowance open. Repeat to add the remaining strips.

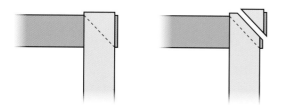

4 Cut one end of the binding strip at a 45° angle. Fold the binding in half lengthwise, wrong sides together and aligning the raw edges; press.

5 Place the binding on the front of the quilt with the raw edges aligned. Start away from a corner.

6 Using a walking foot and a ¼" seam allowance, stitch the binding in place, leaving a 6" to 8" tail at the beginning. When you near the corner, stop and make a mark ¼" away from the edge. You can do this easily by folding the binding up to expose ¼" for the quilt top, and then creasing the binding.

7 Stitch until you reach the ¼" mark; turn the quilt and sew off the edge at a 45° angle.

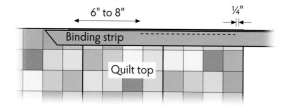

8 Remove the quilt from the machine; rotate it so that you're ready to stitch down the next side. Flip the binding strip up and away from the quilt, creating a 45° angle at the corner. Fold the binding back down, covering the corner with the excess bulk underneath. This will create the miter on the quilt front.

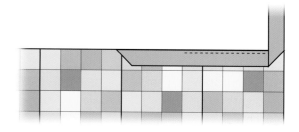

9 Ensure the binding and quilt raw edges are aligned. Begin sewing at the binding fold at the top edge and continue sewing until you are ¼" from the next corner; sew off the edge as before. Repeat the folding and stitching process until you've mitered each corner and are about 10" from where you began stitching. Backstitch and remove the quilt from the machine.

10 Overlap the ending tail over the beginning tail. Trim the end so it overlaps the beginning about 6" to 8".

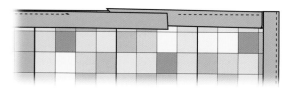

11 Open the tails and place the beginning tail inside the ending tail. Make sure that both tails are flat. Mark the 45° line of the beginning tail on the ending tail.

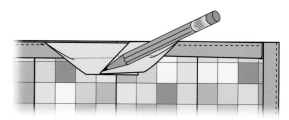

12 Fold the beginning tail back and out of the way. Cut the ending tail parallel and ½" to the right of the marked line.

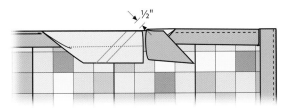

13 Scrunch your quilt out of the way and pin the tails right sides together, offsetting the angled edges slightly. A small triangle of fabric will extend past each side. Sew the ends together. Finger press the seam allowances open.

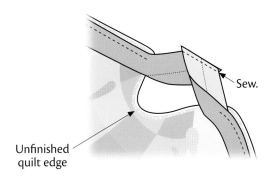

Sew.

Unfinished quilt edge

14 Refold the binding and finish stitching it in place.

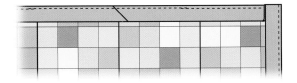

15 From the front of the quilt, gently iron the attached binding away from the quilt top. This makes it easier to fold over to the back.

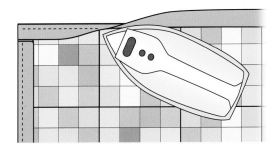

16 Fold the binding over to the back and hold it in place with binding clips. As you come to each corner, fold the binding at a 45° angle to create a miter. Clip or pin the corners in place.

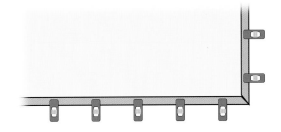

17 Refer to "Finishing By Hand" below or "Finishing By Machine" on page 110 to stitch the binding in place.

Finishing By Hand

I like curling up on the couch to bind by hand while enjoying some family TV time. I almost always bind my quilts by hand and love the clean look of a hand-stitched finish. I usually have leftover matching thread in the bobbin from attaching the binding to the quilt and use it to stitch down the binding.

1 Thread a hand-sewing needle with a 12" to 15" length of thread and knot one of the ends.

2 Starting on one of the quilt sides, insert your needle into the fold of the binding. Hide your knot under the fold of the binding and pull the thread taut, ready to stitch. I work with the quilt spread out in front of me, sewing from right to left with the binding closest to me.

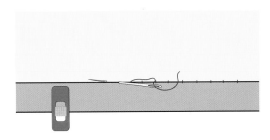

■ Choose a decorative stitch with contrasting bindings (left) or a straight stitch when the border, binding, and backing match (right).

3 Pick up a few threads of the backing fabric next to the binding, and then insert the needle back through the fold of the binding, pulling the thread all the way through as you go. Insert the needle into the backing fabric again, about ⅛" to ¼" away from the last stitch, then insert it again through the binding fold. Continue in this manner to attach the binding to the quilt, sewing up and into the mitered corners as you go. Slip the needle through to the front of the quilt and sew the miters closed on the front as well. When you near the end of a length of thread, knot it and pop it through to the batting layer.

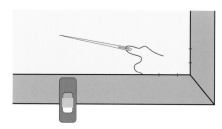

Finishing by Machine

When machine stitching the binding in place, I stitch from the back of the quilt, so the bobbin thread will show on the front of the quilt. Therefore, I match my thread color to my binding and choose either a decorative stitch or a straight stitch.

Decorative Stitching

1 Bring both thread tails to the surface of the quilt. Take a few straight stitches in place, Then, set the decorative stitch on your machine and begin stitching, letting the machine form the design of the stitch over the folded edge of the binding.

2 Stitch slowly, allowing the machine to do its work. When you near a corner, leave the needle down in the quilt and pivot the quilt, letting the decorative design stitch over the corners.

3 When you finish stitching the binding, bring both threads to the top and make a knot, popping it into the batting to secure the threads.

Straight Stitching

Straight stitching works best when the border fabric matches the binding fabric. In case there are any wobbles, it won't be as noticeable.

1 Working from the back of the quilt, stitch just to the right of the binding folded edge. Don't try to stitch in the ditch because it's too difficult to match up on the front.

2 You want to feel that the needle is stitching through both binding layers on the back and the front. Check the front. If you've missed the edge of the binding on the front, try to give yourself a little bit more stitching allowance on the back.

3 Stitch the entire perimeter of the quilt, rotating the quilt at the corners.

4 When you finish stitching the binding, bring both threads to the top and make a knot, popping it into the batting to secure the threads.

SIGNING YOUR QUILT

When your quilt is finished, I hope you'll want to sign it and share it! Signing your quilt can be as simple as writing your name on the back of the quilt with a permanent fabric marker, or as elaborate as making up an extra quilt block with hand-embroidered words.

I'm pretty utilitarian when it comes to labels. I include basic information on my labels: the name of the quilt, the year it was made, my name and city, and the name of the recipient if it's a gift. I usually write the pertinent information with a fabric marker on a piece of plain fabric and sew it to the back corner of the quilt. You can sew a piece of fabric to the back of the quilt before quilting, or you can add it as an afterthought once the quilt is finished (this is the method I usually choose). To save time hand stitching, you can add the label before the binding is sewn so that some of it is tucked into the seam allowances.

Quilt back

Pearl Gray
by Christa Watson
Las Vegas, Nevada
2014

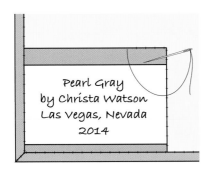

Pearl Gray
by Christa Watson
Las Vegas, Nevada
2014

ADDING A HANGING SLEEVE

If you want to hang your quilt on a wall, or display it in a quilt show, you'll need to add a hanging sleeve to the back. A standard size is 4" wide by the width of the quilt. I use this method to sew a sleeve to the back of the quilt once the binding has been sewn to the front of the quilt, but *before* it's been folded over and stitched in place.

1. Cut a strip of fabric 8½" wide and ½" shorter than the width of the quilt.

2. Fold the ends under ¼" twice and stitch them in place.

¼"

Hem the ends.

3. Fold the fabric strip in half lengthwise, wrong sides together, and press the fold.

4. On the quilt back, pin the folded strip to the top edge of the quilt, aligning the raw edges. Baste the sleeve in place slightly less than ¼" from the raw edges.

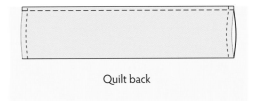

Quilt back

5. Pin the bottom edge of the sleeve in place, and then hand stitch to secure the sleeve to the backing, making sure not to stitch through to the front of the quilt.

6. Fold the binding over to the back and stitch it in place by hand or machine to enclose the sleeve raw edges.

Acknowledgments

I'd like to thank the following companies for providing products for me to make these quilts.

ANDOVER FABRICS
AndoverFabrics.com

AURIFIL (THREAD)
Aurifil.com

CREATIVE GRIDS (RULERS)
CreativeGridsusa.com

MODA (FABRICS)
UnitedNotions.com

PELLON (BATTING)
PellonProjects.com

QUILTERS DREAM BATTING
QuiltersDreamBatting.com

RILEY BLAKE DESIGNS (FABRICS)
RileyBlakeDesigns.com

ROBERT KAUFMAN FABRICS
RobertKaufman.com

WESTMINSTER FIBERS (FABRICS)
WestminsterFibers.com

about the AUXHOR

Christa Watson wanted to be an artist, a business owner, and an ice-cream lady when she grew up. So far she's been able to meet the first two of her goals, but she's still working on that last one!

Her background in traditional quiltmaking led her to enjoy learning every step of the quiltmaking process; her fascination with modern quilts has rekindled her love for the craft. An award-winning quiltmaker, Christa has had designs featured in such magazines as *Quilty, The Quilting Quarterly, Modern Quilts Unlimited, Make Modern, QuiltCon,* and various other publications. She currently designs quilt patterns, teaches workshops, and is an active member of the Modern Quilt Guild, the National Quilting Association, and the American Quilter's Society.

Christa enjoys being a wife to her husband and a mom to her three kids, who all think it's normal to have a house full of fabric. You can keep up with her daily antics on Instagram @christaquilts and see more of her work on her website at ChristaQuilts.com.